2ND EDITION REVISED & EXPANDED

795.415
R329e2

3182 1479

THE EXTRA EDGE IN PLAY
at bridge

MASTER POINT PRESS | TORONTO

Master Point Press
331 Douglas Ave.
Toronto, Ontario, Canada
M5M 1H2
(416) 781-0351
Website: http://www.masterpointpress.com
Email: info@masterpointpress.com

Library and Archives Canada Cataloguing in Publication

Reese, Terence
          The extra edge in play at bridge / written by Terence Reese &
Julian Pottage.

Previously published under title: The extra edge in play.

ISBN 1-894154-97-5

1. Contract bridge. I. Pottage, Julian II. Title.

GV1282.3.R442 2005   795.4'15   C2005-905193-0

Editor	Ray Lee
Cover and interior design	Olena S. Sullivan/New Mediatrix
Interior format	Luise Lee
Copyediting	Suzanne Hocking

Printed in Canada by Webcom Ltd.

1 2 3 4 5 6 7   09 08 07 06 05

Introduction

Bobby Fischer, the reclusive chess champion, once said: 'You have found a good move — fine — now look for a better one.' The same advice applies in bridge. If you settle for second best, you will not achieve your full potential. Through a series of problems that we believe are both fresh and a genuine test of skill, we want to offer you the chance to become accustomed to looking for that extra edge. Whether or not you find the best answers first time round, you will surely develop new ways of thinking to strengthen your game.

Among the techniques you will encounter are: how to make the most of your chances in a single suit; how to force opponents to lead a key suit for you; how to read the cards in the light of the bidding; how to achieve the right timing; how to deceive your opponents about your actual holding.

As this is a book about card play, we have generally kept the bidding simple — using the type of methods you might meet at the rubber bridge table in London. On those occasions when only someone used to a certain system or style (five-card majors and a strong notrump, for example) might feel at home with the bidding, we have included an explanation.

Problem number one is fairly easy and number seventy-six rather tricky, but the others appear in random order. After all, when you are playing at the table there is nobody to warn you that a particular deal is more difficult than it looks, is there?

Terence Reese 1994
Julian Pottage 2005

Acknowledgments

The authors are indebted to Hugh Kelsey and Peter Crawley for their help in editing the original edition of this book.

The authors also owe their gratitude to Peter Burrows, Maureen Dennison, Mark Horton, Ray Lee and Alwyn Reese for playing a part in enabling this new, expanded and improved edition to appear in print.

William Bailey, whose Deep Finesse software helped so much with the additional material and in verifying the accuracy of the original analysis, also deserves a mention. The same applies to the various people, both named and unnamed, who first brought some of the deals to the authors' attention.

Contents

Slow but Fairly Sure

```
            ♠ 2
            ♡ 10 8
            ◇ A 5 3
            ♣ K Q J 9 7 5 2

                  ┌─────────┐
                  │    N    │
  ◇ 9 led         │ W     E │
                  │    S    │
                  └─────────┘

            ♠ Q J 7 5 4 3
            ♡ A K Q
            ◇ K Q J 2
            ♣ —
```

Dealer North
Both vul.

WEST	NORTH	EAST	SOUTH
	1♣	pass	1♠
pass	2♣	pass	2◇
pass	3♣	pass	3NT
all pass			

Your 2◇, being a change of suit rebid, created a one-round force, and the final contract seems reasonable.

Since there are insufficient entries to establish and run the club suit, you will need to play on the spades. How will you do this after winning the diamond lead in one hand or the other?

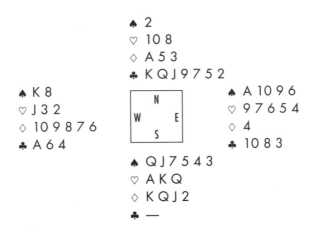

♠ 2
♡ 10 8
◇ A 5 3
♣ K Q J 9 7 5 2

♠ K 8
♡ J 3 2
◇ 10 9 8 7 6
♣ A 6 4

N
W E
S

♠ A 10 9 6
♡ 9 7 6 5 4
◇ 4
♣ 10 8 3

♠ Q J 7 5 4 3
♡ A K Q
◇ K Q J 2
♣ —

You are in 3NT and West has led the nine of diamonds. (Many players treat the ten as a 'strong' lead.)

You can afford to lose three spades, so no problem arises if the suit breaks 3-3. You must concentrate on the 4-2 divisions.

The most critical situation is where West has a doubleton, as in the diagram. It would be a mistake, as you see, to take the first trick in dummy and lead low to the jack and king; that way you would lose four spade tricks. It works better to play low from your hand on both the first and second round.

Since you intend to duck in both hands, it should make no difference whether you begin with the two of spades from dummy or the three from your hand. We admit that if East held something like A-K-10-8 you would do better to lead from dummy and win with the queen or jack. However, you intend to play small from hand: if East has four spades, he is more likely to hold A-10-x-x *or* K-10-x-x than precisely A-K-10-x.

There are some other interesting plays of this kind. With a small singleton opposite your A-J-10-x-x-x, for example, the best play for four tricks is the ace (or ideally up to the ace) followed by a low card. This succeeds against K-x or Q-x on either side, a better chance than finding K-Q-x-x on your right.

No Genius

```
        ♠ 9 7 6 4
        ♡ Q
        ◇ A J 10 6
        ♣ A K 8 3

              N
◇ K led    W     E
              S

        ♠ A K J 10 8
        ♡ A J 5
        ◇ 9 2
        ♣ J 6 5
```

Dealer South
N–S vul.

WEST	NORTH	EAST	SOUTH
			1♠
pass	4♣	pass	4♡
pass	5♡	pass	6♠
all pass			

North's 4♣ was a conventional bid (from the days before splinters) indicating spade support, an unspecified singleton and two aces. With his moderate spades, it might have been wiser to begin with 2♣ or 2◇. Since he had already shown two aces, the bid of five hearts suggested a singleton heart.

The king of diamonds lead means there will be a discard for the losing club, but how will you tackle the trump suit?

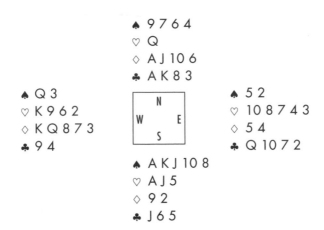

```
              ♠ 9 7 6 4
              ♡ Q
              ◇ A J 10 6
              ♣ A K 8 3
♠ Q 3                          ♠ 5 2
♡ K 9 6 2        N             ♡ 10 8 7 4 3
◇ K Q 8 7 3   W     E          ◇ 5 4
♣ 9 4            S             ♣ Q 10 7 2
              ♠ A K J 10 8
              ♡ A J 5
              ◇ 9 2
              ♣ J 6 5
```

You play in 6♠ and West leads the diamond king. You will not have to worry about the third club now, but you may well have to take a view in the trump suit.

A 3-1 break occurs more often than a 2-2 break, but if you cash the ace, the singleton queen might fall. This means that if the queen does not drop on the first round then the odds are almost even on whether she will do so on the second.

Since West appears more likely than East to hold length in diamonds, you could reasonably play East for three spades to the queen, but on such occasions there is sometimes a way to entrap a non-expert defender. Take the first diamond and play one straight back. Then win a club return in dummy and lead the master jack of diamonds. At this point, many players in the East position would ruff with a confident air, solving all your problems.

Of course, it wouldn't be good play for East to ruff: he should ask himself why declarer has not played on trumps at once. If East nonchalantly discards, declarer will surely feel inclined to place him with an original Q-x-x. So really it comes down to a question of how South estimates his opponent.

Test Case

♠ 9 6 4 3
♡ K 8 5 3
◇ A Q
♣ A 7 5

```
      N
  W       E
      S
```

♠A led

♠ Q J 2
♡ A Q 9 7 6 2
◇ J 7
♣ K 4

Dealer North
Neither vul.

WEST	NORTH	EAST	SOUTH
	1NT[1]	pass	3♡
pass	4♣	pass	4♡
all pass			

1. 12-14

Over 3♡ North has good enough support to show willingness for a slam with an advance cuebid of 4♣, but you are not interested.

West begins with the ace and king of spades, East throwing a small diamond on the second round. East ruffs the third round of spades and then leads the jack of clubs. How should you plan the play?

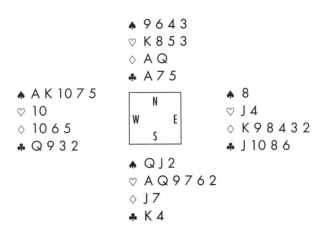

♠ 9 6 4 3
♡ K 8 5 3
◇ A Q
♣ A 7 5

♠ A K 10 7 5
♡ 10
◇ 10 6 5
♣ Q 9 3 2

♠ 8
♡ J 4
◇ K 9 8 4 3 2
♣ J 10 8 6

♠ Q J 2
♡ A Q 9 7 6 2
◇ J 7
♣ K 4

You play in 4♡. The defenders take two spades and their ruff; East then exits with the jack of clubs.

As West has spade length, East is likely to hold the ◇K. You should win with the king of clubs, cash dummy's ace of diamonds, then run the trumps, arriving at this position:

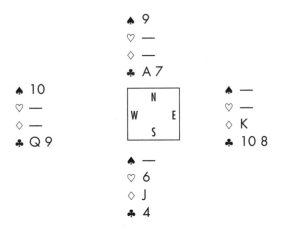

♠ 9
♡ —
◇ —
♣ A 7

♠ 10
♡ —
◇ —
♣ Q 9

♠ —
♡ —
◇ K
♣ 10 8

♠ —
♡ 6
◇ J
♣ 4

Now the last trump effects a double squeeze.

When you cashed the ace of diamonds to make your jack available as a threat against the king, this was a *Vienna Coup*.

Optimist

```
        ♠ A J 9
        ♡ 8 7 6
        ◇ K 5
        ♣ K 7 5 4 2

              ┌─────────┐
              │    N    │
◇ 4 led       │ W     E │
              │    S    │
              └─────────┘

        ♠ K Q 10 8 3
        ♡ A 10 4 2
        ◇ 8 7
        ♣ A J
```

Dealer South
Neither vul.

WEST	NORTH	EAST	SOUTH
			1♠
pass	2♣	pass	2♡
pass	3♠	pass	4♠
all pass			

In traditional Acol, a change of suit response of 2♣ does not promise a great hand and North subsequently needed to give jump preference to show three-card spade support and invite game. In Standard American, North would rebid 2♠ knowing you would bid again.

West leads the four of diamonds and you put up dummy's king. East takes two tricks with the ace and jack, then shifts to the five of hearts. Clearly, you will need to set up some club winners for heart discards. How do you proceed?

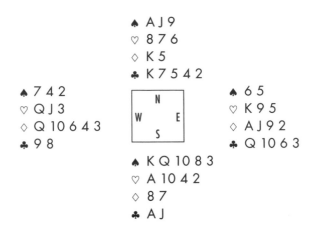

```
                 ♠ A J 9
                 ♡ 8 7 6
                 ◇ K 5
                 ♣ K 7 5 4 2
   ♠ 7 4 2          ┌─────────┐      ♠ 6 5
   ♡ Q J 3          │    N    │      ♡ K 9 5
   ◇ Q 10 6 4 3     │ W     E │      ◇ A J 9 2
   ♣ 9 8            │    S    │      ♣ Q 10 6 3
                    └─────────┘
                 ♠ K Q 10 8 3
                 ♡ A 10 4 2
                 ◇ 8 7
                 ♣ A J
```

You are in 4♠ and West leads a small diamond. East cashes two diamond tricks and shifts to the five of hearts.

This deal is a little deceptive. To begin with, ducking the first heart cannot help you to make the contract, because if you lose another trick after that you will go down anyway. If you put up the ace, you may finish with eleven tricks.

After you have won the first heart, a possible line is to take three rounds of clubs, ruffing the third. This will bring in ten tricks when the spades break 3-2 and the clubs 3-3.

However, this is too optimistic. You do better, after the ace of hearts, to cross to dummy and finesse the jack of clubs. You risk going two down, if West produces the queen, but as the cards lie, this sets you on the right path — you unblock the ace of clubs, cross back to dummy and ruff a club to make five spades, four clubs and a heart. It also works when East has a doubleton ♣Q-x; again, you can set up four club tricks.

Finally — not easy to foresee — you can succeed when East holds ♣Q-x-x and *four* trumps. After the second round of spades, you play good clubs from the table. When East ruffs, you over-ruff and return to dummy to make a fourth club trick.

```
              ♠ Q 6
              ♡ 7 5 3
              ◇ K 8 7 4 2
              ♣ A K J

                   ┌─────────┐
                   │    N    │
   ♡ 4 led         │ W     E │
                   │    S    │
                   └─────────┘

              ♠ A 8 3
              ♡ A 10 2
              ◇ Q 9 6 3
              ♣ Q 10 4
```

Dealer South
E–W vul.

WEST	NORTH	EAST	SOUTH
			1NT[1]
pass	3NT	all pass	

1. 12-14

Some people decide whether to open the bidding by adding their high card points to the number of cards in their two longest suits. This normally produces the result that they open any hand with 12 HCP upwards unless it has a 4333 shape. Although the idea has merit, striking the first blow, especially when you can do so with some preemptive effect, often works well.

Against your normal 3NT contract, West leads the four of hearts and East plays the queen. You probably cannot afford to lose two diamonds. What is your strategy?

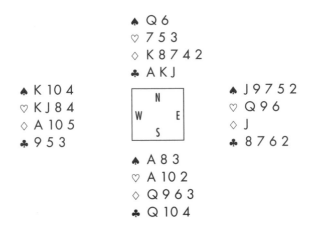

```
              ♠ Q 6
              ♡ 7 5 3
              ◇ K 8 7 4 2
              ♣ A K J
♠ K 10 4      ┌─────────┐      ♠ J 9 7 5 2
♡ K J 8 4     │    N    │      ♡ Q 9 6
◇ A 10 5      │ W     E │      ◇ J
♣ 9 5 3       │    S    │      ♣ 8 7 6 2
              └─────────┘
              ♠ A 8 3
              ♡ A 10 2
              ◇ Q 9 6 3
              ♣ Q 10 4
```

You are playing in 3NT and West leads the four of hearts to his partner's queen.

The play to the first trick needs consideration. If you duck, then as the cards lie, a spade switch from East would prove threatening: you would have to duck and the opponents might then revert to hearts. This sequence of plays does not sound very likely, but if you take West's four of hearts as fourth best, holding up the ace serves no purpose.

You win with the ace of hearts, therefore, and now have to consider which defender might hold three diamonds to the ace. You have a clue to this. It would appear that West has led from a four-card suit, so unless he is precisely 4-4-1-4 — and has chosen to lead a heart — he will not hold a singleton diamond.

Having decided that East is more likely than West to be short in diamonds, you cross to the ♣K and lead a small diamond; this runs to the jack, queen and ace. When you regain the lead, you play the next diamond from hand and West plays low. Now you should finesse, for more than one reason. On restricted choice principles, East's jack is more likely to be single than from J-10. Another point is that if West were not 3-4-3-3 he might have led his other four-card suit rather than a heart from K-J-x-x.

Deep Sea

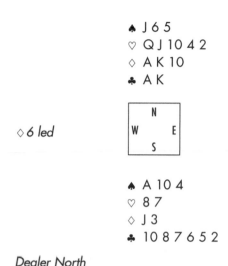

♠ J 6 5
♡ Q J 10 4 2
◇ A K 10
♣ A K

◇ 6 led

♠ A 10 4
♡ 8 7
◇ J 3
♣ 10 8 7 6 5 2

Dealer North
Both vul.

WEST	NORTH	EAST	SOUTH
	1♡	pass	1NT
pass	3NT	all pass	

North was clearly too good even for a strong 1NT and, with two tens and a five-card suit, his rebid seems justified. At rubber and teams scoring, it pays to bid close vulnerable games.

West leads a small diamond and you get off to a good start when East plays the two under dummy's ten.

There are still only six tricks on top. Where will you look for the other three? Unless you strike it very lucky, you can forget about bringing in the long clubs. You might manage it in hearts perhaps, or in some kind of combination.

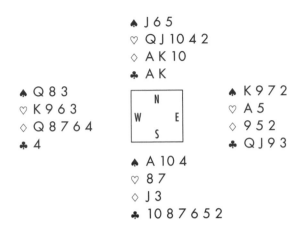

```
                     ♠ J 6 5
                     ♡ Q J 10 4 2
                     ◊ A K 10
                     ♣ A K
  ♠ Q 8 3          ┌──────────┐      ♠ K 9 7 2
  ♡ K 9 6 3        │    N     │      ♡ A 5
  ◊ Q 8 7 6 4      │ W      E │      ◊ 9 5 2
  ♣ 4              │    S     │      ♣ Q J 9 3
                   └──────────┘
                     ♠ A 10 4
                     ♡ 8 7
                     ◊ J 3
                     ♣ 10 8 7 6 5 2
```

You play in 3NT and West leads the six of diamonds. You have to try finessing the ten, and East plays low.

Your only chance to make anything of the long clubs is to bring down a doubleton Q-J. However, even if the queen or jack falls under the ace, you won't know where you stand. You do better to concentrate on the hearts. Begin by overtaking the ◊ 10 with the jack and leading the eight of hearts. You will have to make a decision — whether to play one of dummy's honors — if West plays one of the three smallest cards — the six, five or three.

There is not a great deal in it, but as you may not get another convenient chance to lead hearts from hand, the probabilities say to run the eight. This loses if West has x-x-x, A-x-x, or K-x-x, in each case without the nine. It will gain whenever West holds A-9-x-x, K-9-x-x, A-K-9-x or 9-x, a more numerous assortment. (Remember that x-x-x, in this context, means precisely 6-5-3.)

With combinations like this, the finesse is frequently superior to playing for a 3-3 split. A well-known example occurs when you hold 10-9 opposite A-K-Q-x-x. To run the ten loses when East holds J-x-x over the long suit but gains when East holds x-x-x-x or x-x. You have to lose a trick either way when East holds J-x.

Novel Theory

♠ K Q J 5
♡ K Q J 6
◇ A J 9
♣ 7 5

♡ 10 led

	N	
W		E
	S	

♠ A 7
♡ A 3
◇ K 10 3
♣ A K 8 6 3 2

Dealer South
Neither vul.

WEST	NORTH	EAST	SOUTH
			2NT
pass	7NT	all pass	

Your 2NT, whilst not classical, seems fair enough in a match-point pairs event where one often ignores minor suits.

West leads the ten of hearts against your grand slam. You have twelve tricks on top and a two-way finesse in diamonds for the thirteenth. What you can do to increase your chances of making a winning decision?

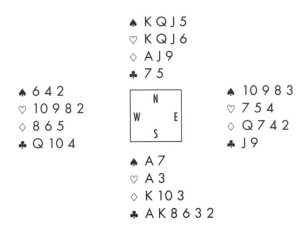

```
              ♠ K Q J 5
              ♡ K Q J 6
              ◇ A J 9
              ♣ 7 5
♠ 6 4 2                          ♠ 10 9 8 3
♡ 10 9 8 2      N                ♡ 7 5 4
◇ 8 6 5       W   E              ◇ Q 7 4 2
♣ Q 10 4        S                ♣ J 9
              ♠ A 7
              ♡ A 3
              ◇ K 10 3
              ♣ A K 8 6 3 2
```

You boldly open 2NT and North raises to 7NT. West leads the ♡10.

When dummy goes down you see that you need a finesse or possibly a show-up squeeze; this isn't nice, especially since, if you fail, partner will ask why you opened 2NT on only 18 points. Can you give yourself anything better than a 50-50 chance?

You should begin by cashing the ♣A-K followed by, say, four spades and two more hearts. You have discarded three clubs already, which makes the discard on the last heart a trifle awkward. You should let go of your last small club so that you will have a two-way finesse in diamonds.

Now, despite the symmetry in the East-West majors, have you any indication about the location of the diamond queen? Yes, but the nature of the clue may not have occurred to you.

The point is that the four of clubs *must* appear on the first two rounds of the suit, and whoever played it figures to hold the missing club, since there are six tripleton holdings including the four and only four doubletons. Thus, East figures to have two clubs and four diamonds, so you gallantly finesse against him.

The point about the four of clubs first appeared in a Bols tip. We find it a novel and interesting idea, worthy of examination.

Second String

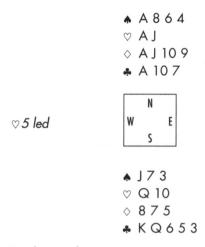

♠ A 8 6 4
♡ A J
◇ A J 10 9
♣ A 10 7

♡ 5 led

N
W   E
S

♠ J 7 3
♡ Q 10
◇ 8 7 5
♣ K Q 6 5 3

Dealer North
Both vul.

WEST	NORTH	EAST	SOUTH
	1◇	pass	1NT
pass	2NT	pass	3NT
all pass			

North's bidding is consistent with a hand too good even for a strong notrump, which made it a very easy decision for you to accept the invitation.

When West leads a small heart you are obliged to let it run and, happily for you, East cannot beat the jack. Five club tricks would give you game, but life is not always like that. How do you set about the play?

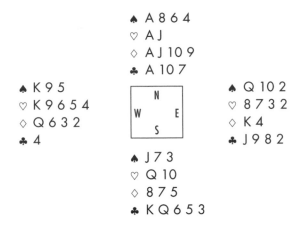

```
              ♠ A 8 6 4
              ♡ A J
              ◇ A J 10 9
              ♣ A 10 7
♠ K 9 5                          ♠ Q 10 2
♡ K 9 6 5 4      N               ♡ 8 7 3 2
◇ Q 6 3 2     W     E            ◇ K 4
♣ 4              S               ♣ J 9 8 2
              ♠ J 7 3
              ♡ Q 10
              ◇ 8 7 5
              ♣ K Q 6 5 3
```

You are in 3NT and you have a choice of where to win the first trick when East cannot beat dummy's jack of hearts.

Five club tricks will see you home for sure but, if the clubs do not run, you will need to make three tricks in diamonds. There is no hurry to test the clubs. Since you may need *three* tricks from the diamonds, you should overtake the heart with the queen and finesse the nine of diamonds. East wins and returns a heart, clearing the suit.

Now play ace and another club, getting the news. No matter. Finesse the ten of diamonds, return to the high club, and finesse again in diamonds. You make game with three diamonds, three clubs and three tricks in the majors.

Can you guess how they went down in the other room? Yes, declarer wasted the heart entry and began with ace and another club before turning to diamonds. When the first suit declined to break and the queen of diamonds was well guarded, he found himself with only eight tricks.

Entries are a precious commodity, especially when the bulk of your side's strength lies in one hand. Squander them at your peril.

∩early There

```
            ♠ K 7 4
            ♡ Q 6 4 2
            ◇ K 9
            ♣ A 10 5 3

                  ┌─────────┐
                  │    N    │
    ♠ Q led       │ W     E │
                  │    S    │
                  └─────────┘

            ♠ A 10 2
            ♡ A K J 10 5
            ◇ A Q
            ♣ K 8 4
```

Dealer South
Neither vul.

WEST	NORTH	EAST	SOUTH
			2NT
pass	3♣	pass	3♡
pass	5♡	pass	6♡
all pass			

Following his Stayman 3♣, North's 5♡ seems well chosen, as it implies values in the other suits and moderate hearts. Also, it avoids any ambiguity: in the absence of an agreement, 4♣, for example, might be either a cuebid or natural, and 4NT could be either an ace inquiry with heart support or quantitative without it.

After the lead, a good chance exists that you will be able to establish a club winner for a spade discard. Also, you might find a way to take advantage of the fact that West cannot safely continue spades. How, then, do you plan for twelve tricks?

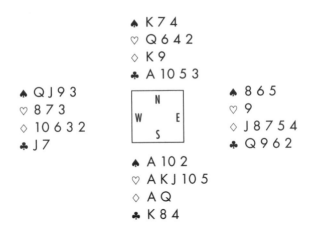

♠ K 7 4
♡ Q 6 4 2
◇ K 9
♣ A 10 5 3

♠ Q J 9 3
♡ 8 7 3
◇ 10 6 3 2
♣ J 7

♠ 8 6 5
♡ 9
◇ J 8 7 5 4
♣ Q 9 6 2

♠ A 10 2
♡ A K J 10 5
◇ A Q
♣ K 8 4

You are in 6♡ and West leads the queen of spades.

The contract is *almost* laydown. Take the ace of spades, draw trumps and cash the diamond winners. Then play the ace of clubs and a club to the eight. If West wins this trick, he cannot safely play a spade (or diamond). He will be endplayed when he holds a doubleton club, as in the diagram.

If West has three clubs, or if East has 9-x, J-x or Q-x (when you will take the king), there will be a discard on dummy's fourth club. If instead West has four or more clubs including the Q-J-9, he may return a club, but playing off all the hearts will squeeze him in the black suits.

Finally, if East has five clubs, you win the second round of the suit and throw West in with the third round of spades, forcing him to concede a ruff and discard.

So can you ever fail? Yes, if East has Q-J-9-x in clubs and you stuck with your original plan to play a third round after the ace and king. However, you *might* change tack and play West for a doubleton, following the ace and king of clubs with king and another spade, again leaving West on play.

Find the Lady

<pre>
                    ♠ K 7 5
                    ♡ K J 10
                    ◇ A Q J 3
                    ♣ A J 7
</pre>

```
              ┌─────────┐
              │    N    │
♠ Q led       │ W     E │
              │    S    │
              └─────────┘
```

<pre>
                    ♠ A 10
                    ♡ A 9 8 7 5 3 2
                    ◇ 8 6 2
                    ♣ K
</pre>

Dealer South
Neither vul.

WEST	NORTH	EAST	SOUTH
			1♡
pass	3◇	pass	3♡
pass	4♣	pass	4♠
pass	6♡	all pass	

The accepted modern style for responder, with a two-suiter of his own, is not to force. So you interpret 4♣ as a cuebid and conclude that your partner has fair support for hearts. Once you bypassed 4◇ (thereby denying the king of diamonds) North settled for the small slam.

West leads the queen of spades and East follows with the three. Knowing the diamond finesse may be wrong, how you play the trumps may prove critical.

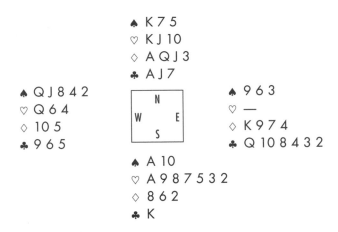

```
                    ♠ K 7 5
                    ♡ K J 10
                    ◇ A Q J 3
                    ♣ A J 7
   ♠ Q J 8 4 2       ┌─────────┐       ♠ 9 6 3
   ♡ Q 6 4           │    N    │       ♡ —
   ◇ 10 5            │ W     E │       ◇ K 9 7 4
   ♣ 9 6 5           │    S    │       ♣ Q 10 8 4 3 2
                     └─────────┘
                    ♠ A 10
                    ♡ A 9 8 7 5 3 2
                    ◇ 8 6 2
                    ♣ K
```

You find your way to the good contract of 6♡ and West leads the
queen of spades, East playing the three.

The diamond finesse may be (and in this book will be) wrong,
so you must consider how to play the trump suit. There is a
slight inference that West holds length in spades — he has two
known cards in the suit, the queen and the jack — and he would
not rush to lead the queen from Q-J-x. On these grounds, you
may feel inclined to begin with a small heart to the king.

As the cards lie, this will cost you the contract and your partner may dispute your reasoning. 'The point is,' he will say, 'that
if East does turn up with three hearts, you will still have excellent chances even if you begin with the ace. You cash the kings
of hearts, clubs and spades, ruff the third spade, then exit with a
heart. There is a good chance now that East will be down to only
diamonds and clubs and will have to give you a twelfth trick
with his return. Besides, if he could exit with a fourth round of
spades, you would know he started with at least three more
major-suit cards than West, so the diamond finesse would stand
an excellent chance of working.'

Wonder Card

♠ 10 9 6 4 3
♡ 8 6 3
♢ K Q
♣ 9 5 4

♢ J led

♠ A K Q 7 2
♡ A 10 5
♢ A 3
♣ A Q 7

Dealer South
E–W vul.

WEST	NORTH	EAST	SOUTH
			2♣
pass	2♢	pass	2NT
pass	3♣	pass	3♠
pass	4♠	all pass	

North's 3♣ was five-card (or puppet) Stayman. North, quite correctly, decided to treat his spades as a four-card suit.

Owing to the mirror distribution, you would prefer to play in 3NT, because in spades you see four possible losers. What is the best hope for making your contract of 4♠ after the diamond lead?

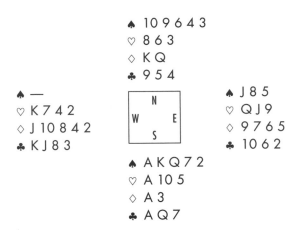

♠ 10 9 6 4 3
♡ 8 6 3
◇ K Q
♣ 9 5 4

♠ —
♡ K 7 4 2
◇ J 10 8 4 2
♣ K J 8 3

N
W   E
S

♠ J 8 5
♡ Q J 9
◇ 9 7 6 5
♣ 10 6 2

♠ A K Q 7 2
♡ A 10 5
◇ A 3
♣ A Q 7

Not having been clever enough to finish in 3NT, you have to make 4♠ after a diamond lead.

The key to the play is to prevent East from gaining the lead twice. First, take the ace of diamonds and then, after drawing trumps (on which West discards two diamonds and a club), cross to the ◇K and lead a heart from dummy. East may play low, in which case you play the ten from hand. West wins and exits with a heart to the jack and ace. When East wins the third round, he will probably try the ten of clubs. You cover with the queen and will have no further problem when West holds the eight and jack of clubs. (You would put up dummy's nine on a low club return, since East is more likely to have been dealt ♣10-8-x *or* J-8-x than J-10-x. On restricted choice principles, the fact that you have seen him play one of the jack or ten doesn't change this.)

With his holding of Q-J-9, East may play high when you lead the first heart from dummy. If he does this, win with the ace, enter dummy again with the fourth round of trumps and lead another heart from the table. If East plays high again and leads the ten of clubs, you need not rely on the club spots. You win with the ace and exit with the ten of hearts to West's king. Take note of what an important card the ten of hearts was here.

Almost Everything Wrong

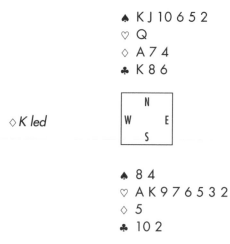

♠ K J 10 6 5 2
♡ Q
◇ A 7 4
♣ K 8 6

◇ K led

```
      N
   W     E
      S
```

♠ 8 4
♡ A K 9 7 6 5 3 2
◇ 5
♣ 10 2

Dealer North
E–W vul.

WEST	NORTH	EAST	SOUTH
	1♠	pass	2♡
pass	2♠	pass	4♡
all pass			

An eight-card suit counts for a lot. Unless you are one of those who play that a two-over-one response creates a game force, you have an automatic response of 2♡.

At worst (barring a 4-0 break in hearts, which is unlikely at the best of times, especially when the opponents hold half the high cards and pass throughout), you could find yourself losing two clubs and two spades in this heart game. After a diamond lead, how might you escape that unhappy fate?

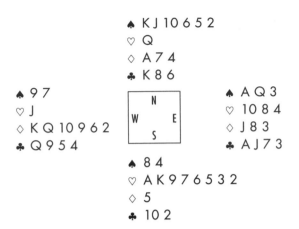

♠ K J 10 6 5 2
♡ Q
◇ A 7 4
♣ K 8 6

♠ 9 7
♡ J
◇ K Q 10 9 6 2
♣ Q 9 5 4

♠ A Q 3
♡ 10 8 4
◇ J 8 3
♣ A J 7 3

♠ 8 4
♡ A K 9 7 6 5 3 2
◇ 5
♣ 10 2

You are in 4♡ and West leads the king of diamonds.

Each year England, Scotland, Wales, Northern Ireland (and now the Republic of Ireland) compete in a home international series. In one of these matches South reasoned on these lines: after cashing the queen of hearts, I'll come over to hand with a diamond ruff, draw trumps, and begin with a club to the king. If this loses to the ace, I'll play West for the ace of spades.

As you see, this plan did not quite work! Nor did the line chosen at the other table fare any better. Also working on the theory of split aces, the declarer started the same way but played on spades before clubs. East scored two spade tricks and got off play with a diamond.

A better line is to attempt an elimination. After taking the ◇A, ruff a diamond, cross to the queen of hearts, and ruff another diamond. After drawing trumps, lead a spade to the jack. East wins with the queen but, having no more diamonds, can only cash his two aces. This line would have failed if East had held the queen of spades and the ace of clubs, while West held the ace of spades; all the same, it would have provided an extra chance.

```
        ♠ 10 9 8 5
        ♡ A 9 7 4
        ◇ 9 2
        ♣ A K 8
```

	N	
♣ Q led	W E	
	S	

```
        ♠ A J
        ♡ J 8 6 5 3 2
        ◇ K 6 5
        ♣ 6 2
```

Dealer West
E–W vul.

WEST	NORTH	EAST	SOUTH
1◇	dbl	1♠	4♡
all pass			

On the bidding, the diamond ace surely sits over the king (and this would perhaps suggest that you should have bid only 3♡). You will therefore need to do something with the spades or develop an endplay, forcing a lead up to the king of diamonds. You will also have to assume a 2-1 trump split.

What are your plans when West leads a neutral queen of clubs?

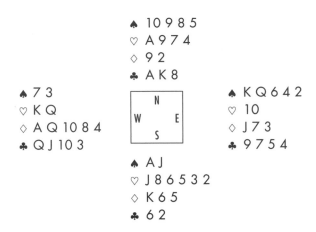

```
                    ♠ 10 9 8 5
                    ♡ A 9 7 4
                    ◇ 9 2
                    ♣ A K 8
  ♠ 7 3                               ♠ K Q 6 4 2
  ♡ K Q                               ♡ 10
  ◇ A Q 10 8 4                        ◇ J 7 3
  ♣ Q J 10 3                          ♣ 9 7 5 4
                    ♠ A J
                    ♡ J 8 6 5 3 2
                    ◇ K 6 5
                    ♣ 6 2
```

You play in 4♡ after West opened 1◇, North doubled, and East bid 1♠. West leads the ♣Q.

On the surface, there are four losers — one in spades, one in hearts and two in diamonds. Finding West with a singleton spade sounds like one possibility; this would allow you to cash the ace of spades, eliminate the clubs, and give West the lead on the second round of hearts. On the whole, though, West is more likely to hold a doubleton spade and East the ♠K-Q.

In this case you will have to devise a way to prevent East from gaining the lead. As a start, let West hold the first trick with the queen of clubs! Enlivened by this success, West may decide to switch to a heart. Win with the ace and lead a small spade from the table, on which East may go in with the ♠Q. Win with the ace, take two rounds of clubs, discarding the ♠J, and take the ruffing finesse through East. If he covers the second spade, ruff and give West the lead in trumps.

You may say: suppose East follows small when you lead the small spade from dummy; after the jack wins, that will leave you with only nine tricks — two spades, five hearts and two clubs. In this event, as in the previous sequence, you can cash the ♡A, two clubs, the ♠A and exit with a heart.

Fair Exchange

```
      ♠ A J 6 2
      ♡ K
      ◇ J 6 2
      ♣ K J 9 7 3

            ┌─────────┐
            │    N    │
  ♣A led    │ W     E │
            │    S    │
            └─────────┘

      ♠ 10 7 5 4 3
      ♡ A Q 10
      ◇ A 5
      ♣ Q 10 2
```

Dealer North
Both vul.

WEST	NORTH	EAST	SOUTH
	1♣	pass	1♠
pass	2♠	pass	4♠
all pass			

In the classic version of the losing trick count, the South hand contains only seven losers. Since you wouldn't want to bid 3NT and have your partner place you with only four spades, this justifies your leap to the spade game.

West leads the ace of clubs, a suspicious choice given that dummy has bid the suit, and East plays the four. West follows with a small diamond, which runs to the ten and ace.

Even if you play the trumps for one loser, it looks as though you may lose a club, a spade, a diamond and a ruff. How will you avoid this?

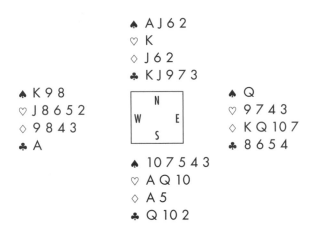

```
                    ♠ A J 6 2
                    ♡ K
                    ◇ J 6 2
                    ♣ K J 9 7 3
♠ K 9 8          ┌──────────┐      ♠ Q
♡ J 8 6 5 2      │    N     │      ♡ 9 7 4 3
◇ 9 8 4 3        │ W      E │      ◇ K Q 10 7
♣ A              │    S     │      ♣ 8 6 5 4
                 └──────────┘
                    ♠ 10 7 5 4 3
                    ♡ A Q 10
                    ◇ A 5
                    ♣ Q 10 2
```

You play in 4♠ after North has opened 1♣. West leads the ace of clubs and switches to a diamond, which you win with the ace.

West's lead of a (probable) singleton ace of dummy's suit is not, in general, an attractive play. This means you can feel fairly sure that he holds something like K-x-x of spades and will have hopes of obtaining a ruff if he can find an entry to his partner's hand. Preparing to accept the loss if West holds K-Q-x, you begin with a spade to the ace; this brings down the queen from East, which confirms your original suspicion.

How will you now prevent West from gaining entry in trumps and putting his partner in with a diamond to give him a club ruff? You'll be annoyed if you haven't seen it! Play the king of hearts to the ace, cash the queen and follow with the ten, discarding two diamonds from dummy. Happily for you, West has the jack of hearts, so you exchange a diamond loser for a heart loser and leave the defenders fuming.

The loser-on-loser play has applications other than cutting the link between the defenders: to ruff a suit that can't be over-ruffed rather than one that can, to endplay an opponent or to rectify the count for a squeeze. Keep a look out for it.

Pressure Point

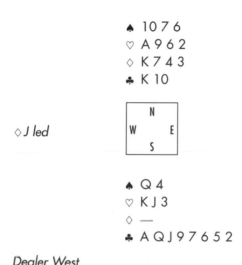

```
              ♠ 10 7 6
              ♡ A 9 6 2
              ◇ K 7 4 3
              ♣ K 10
                  ┌─────┐
                  │  N  │
  ◇ J led         │ W  E│
                  │  S  │
                  └─────┘
              ♠ Q 4
              ♡ K J 3
              ◇ —
              ♣ A Q J 9 7 6 5 2
```

Dealer West
Both vul.

WEST	NORTH	EAST	SOUTH
2◇	pass	2♡	3♣
pass	4♣	pass	5♣
all pass			

West's 2◇ opening is a 'Multi', usually a weak hand with a six-card major. East's 2♡ acts as a relay, to play if West holds hearts. One feature that makes a Multi difficult to counter is that if the opponents do not bid a real suit, you have no cuebid. North may have wished to investigate 3NT but he had no sensible way to do so. This may be fortunate, as it looks like the defenders might have taken eleven or twelve tricks!

It seems more than likely, in view of the heart length between the two hands, that West's suit is spades. How will you play for 5♣ when he leads the jack of diamonds?

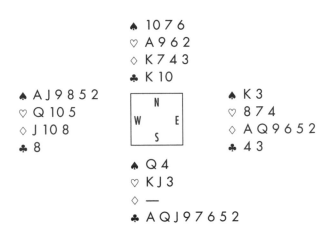

```
                    ♠ 10 7 6
                    ♡ A 9 6 2
                    ◊ K 7 4 3
                    ♣ K 10
    ♠ A J 9 8 5 2      ┌─────────┐      ♠ K 3
    ♡ Q 10 5           │    N    │      ♡ 8 7 4
    ◊ J 10 8           │ W     E │      ◊ A Q 9 6 5 2
    ♣ 8                │    S    │      ♣ 4 3
                       └─────────┘
                    ♠ Q 4
                    ♡ K J 3
                    ◊ —
                    ♣ A Q J 9 7 6 5 2
```

You play in 5♣ after West has opened with a 'Multi' 2◊, equivalent here to a weak two in spades. West leads the jack of diamonds.

It seems to be a matter of determining who has the queen of hearts. If East has this card, a simple finesse will win, or you could squeeze him in hearts and diamonds. If it is West who has the queen of hearts, you might squeeze him in the majors, but the fact that three rounds of spades will destroy dummy's menace card makes life difficult.

Fortunately, there is a neat way to overcome this problem. Don't ruff the first diamond! Instead, discard a spade. If West continues diamonds, ruff and play the queen of spades. Later you will ruff dummy's second spade and play off the trumps. West, down to the ♠A and ♡Q-x-x, will have to let go a heart, and East, with the ◊A and only small hearts, will also come down to a doubleton heart.

It is true that West might, at some point, lead a small spade to the king; then if East returned a heart, you should go up with the king. Also, East might overtake the first diamond, threatening to lead hearts twice and so forcing you to ruff the first round; still, he cannot prevent you from later ducking a diamond to West.

Nothing Lost

```
        ♠ K 8 3
        ♡ 7 2
        ◊ J 9 3
        ♣ A 6 5 3 2
```

```
              ┌─────────┐
              │    N    │
   ♣ K led    │ W     E │
              │    S    │
              └─────────┘
```

```
        ♠ A 7 4
        ♡ K Q J 10 9
        ◊ A Q 10 8
        ♣ 10
```

Dealer South
Neither vul.

WEST	NORTH	EAST	SOUTH
			1♡
pass	1NT	pass	2◊
pass	2♡	pass	2♠
pass	3♣	pass	3♡
pass	4♡	all pass	

On this sort of deal in a pairs event people would reach many different contracts. Four hearts looks as good as any.

When West leads a club, declarer sees that he can afford to lose a heart, a spade and a diamond. Unfortunately, there may be problems of control. How do you set about the play?

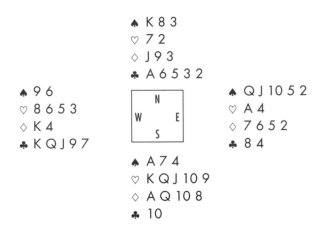

♠ K 8 3
♡ 7 2
◇ J 9 3
♣ A 6 5 3 2

♠ 9 6
♡ 8 6 5 3
◇ K 4
♣ K Q J 9 7

♠ Q J 10 5 2
♡ A 4
◇ 7 6 5 2
♣ 8 4

♠ A 7 4
♡ K Q J 10 9
◇ A Q 10 8
♣ 10

You are in 4♡ and West leads the king of clubs.

You can afford to lose a heart, a spade and a diamond, but a 4-2 break in trumps will create a problem. Thus if you win the club lead, knock out the ace of hearts, and ruff the next club lead, you will soon lose control as the cards lie. Nor does it help to take the diamond finesse before playing trumps as then you run into a ruff.

Well, perhaps the clubs will divide 5-2 (more likely than 6-1, especially in view of West's failure to overcall). In this case, you won't lose anything if you duck the first club, because the ace of clubs will always provide a discard for the third round of spades.

You win the second club, pitching your spade loser, and play on trumps. When East takes the ace, he will exit with the queen of spades. When you have drawn trumps and crossed to the king of spades you will be running the nine of diamonds for an over-trick.

The concept of holding back a winner to disrupt the enemy communications is well known in notrump contracts, but players often overlook its application in suit contracts. A variation can be refusing to ruff and you should watch out for this as well.

fearless fred

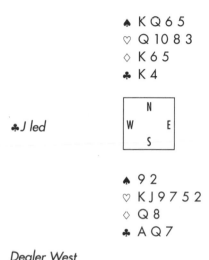

♠ K Q 6 5
♡ Q 10 8 3
◇ K 6 5
♣ K 4

♣J led

♠ 9 2
♡ K J 9 7 5 2
◇ Q 8
♣ A Q 7

Dealer West
Neither vul.

WEST	NORTH	EAST	SOUTH
2♠	pass	pass	3♡
pass	4♡	all pass	

West, who began with a weak two-bid, indicating a six-card suit in a hand too weak in high cards for an opening one-bid, leads the jack of clubs.

There are three aces missing and, unless East turns up with a singleton trump, the danger of a spade ruff looms large. What can do you do to avoid it?

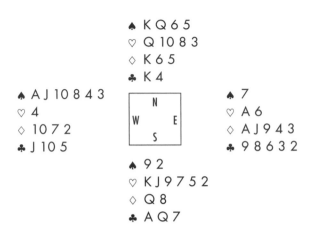

```
              ♠ K Q 6 5
              ♡ Q 10 8 3
              ◇ K 6 5
              ♣ K 4
♠ A J 10 8 4 3    ┌─────────┐    ♠ 7
♡ 4               │    N    │    ♡ A 6
◇ 10 7 2          │ W     E │    ◇ A J 9 4 3
♣ J 10 5          │    S    │    ♣ 9 8 6 3 2
                  └─────────┘
              ♠ 9 2
              ♡ K J 9 7 5 2
              ◇ Q 8
              ♣ A Q 7
```

You play in 4♡ after West has opened with a weak 2♠. West leads the jack of clubs.

Both sides may have an opportunity for clever play on this deal. If you play on hearts at once, East, with his singleton spade, can obtain a ruff. The best plan to avert this danger is to win with the ace of clubs and ride into the valley of death by leading the nine of spades yourself. West will take his ace and, in all probability, read his partner for a doubleton 7-2. He may then try the ten of diamonds, hoping to find East with A-Q-J-x. (Against opponents who use upside-down count signals, it would be best to lead the ♠2, hoping that East's singleton is lower than the nine, so that West may think he has 9-x doubleton.)

A different, but also instructive, point arises if you were to miss the point of attacking spades. Suppose instead that you win the first trick with dummy's king of clubs and try a sly ten of hearts from the table. Now East should go up with the ace but not lead the seven of spades just yet. Instead, he should help West by first cashing the ◇A, which on the bidding can't be a singleton. Then West, when he wins with the ♠A, will know that his partner does not hold the ◇A-Q, but wants a spade ruff.

As declarer, too, you should remember to nurture partner. Rather than shaking your head or saying that you disapprove of partner's bidding, say a polite 'thank you' when he puts down dummy. Also, try not to leave winners stranded on the table!

Choice of Three

♠ Q J 4
♡ 9 5 3 2
♢ Q J 5
♣ A 5 2

♠ 8 led

♠ A 3
♡ K 6
♢ A K 10 4 3
♣ Q J 10 7

Dealer North
Neither vul.

WEST	NORTH	EAST	SOUTH
	pass	pass	1♢
pass	1♡	pass	2NT
pass	3NT	all pass	

Responding 1♡ on 9-x-x-x seems unattractive but nothing is perfect for North. As an opening 1NT by you would have shown 12-14 at this vulnerability, a 1NT response would carry the risk of a missed game if you had, say, a balanced 16 points. You might have rebid 2♣ but, at matchpoint pairs and facing a passed hand, you reasonably bypassed the suit.

On the lead of the eight of spades (presumably from a weak suit) dummy plays the jack and East encourages with the ten. How should you set about the play?

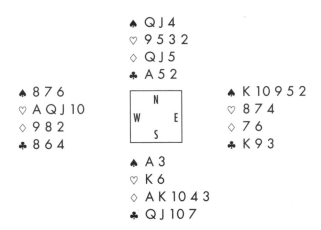

```
              ♠ Q J 4
              ♡ 9 5 3 2
              ◇ Q J 5
              ♣ A 5 2
♠ 8 7 6          ┌─────────┐        ♠ K 10 9 5 2
♡ A Q J 10       │    N    │        ♡ 8 7 4
◇ 9 8 2          │ W     E │        ◇ 7 6
♣ 8 6 4          │    S    │        ♣ K 9 3
                 └─────────┘
              ♠ A 3
              ♡ K 6
              ◇ A K 10 4 3
              ♣ Q J 10 7
```

You play in 3NT and West leads a 'top-of-nothing' eight of spades. On the jack of spades East plays the ten.

If all went well, you might make eleven or twelve tricks, but meanwhile you have only eight on top and appear to need either the club finesse or the ace of hearts with East. You might set about the play in one of three ways.

(1) It is often good tactics to run your long suit and hope to get some indication from the discards. There doesn't seem much point in that here, because the discards are going to prove more awkward for the dummy than for the defenders.

(2) The 'smart crowd' might immediately lead a heart to the king. There is little danger attached to this line and a defender holding something like A-J-x or A-x-x might hold off.

(3) Less adventurous, and quite intelligent because you do not mind losing a club trick to West if he has the king, is to play ace and another club. East may well place you with something like ♣Q-10-x-x and play low from K-x-x or K-x-x-x. If he goes up with the king, he will not necessarily play a heart next. We think this is your best shot.

Third Try

```
          ♠ A 7
          ♡ 10 2
          ◇ A Q J 4 3
          ♣ A 8 5 2

            ┌─────────┐
            │    N    │
♣ K led     │ W     E │
            │    S    │
            └─────────┘

          ♠ 8 4 2
          ♡ K Q J 9 8 6
          ◇ K
          ♣ 6 4 3
```

Dealer North
E–W vul.

WEST	NORTH	EAST	SOUTH
	1◇	pass	1♡
pass	2♣	pass	2♡
pass	3♡	pass	4♡
all pass			

To rebid 2♡ you must possess a decent heart suit, playable opposite a singleton. North, appreciating that 10-x is adequate support and expecting his aces to prove useful, gives a simple raise — an invitation you happily accept.

West leads a hostile king of clubs. Even so, there seem to be plenty of tricks in view and no particular danger. How do you propose to play?

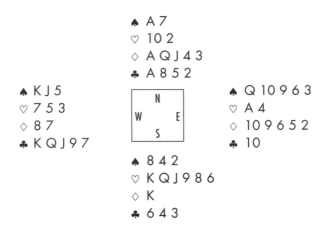

♠ A 7
♥ 10 2
♦ A Q J 4 3
♣ A 8 5 2

♠ K J 5
♥ 7 5 3
♦ 8 7
♣ K Q J 9 7

N
W E
S

♠ Q 10 9 6 3
♥ A 4
♦ 10 9 6 5 2
♣ 10

♠ 8 4 2
♥ K Q J 9 8 6
♦ K
♣ 6 4 3

You play in 4♥ and West leads the king of clubs. You win with the ace, as there is no reason to hold up and ducking would look foolish if East ruffed the next round.

It looks as though you can make ten tricks by way of five trumps, three diamonds and two aces; or you might play for a spade ruff, ducking an early round.

As the cards lie, playing a diamond to the king, a spade to the ace and discarding two clubs on the top diamonds will not work against expert opponents. West will ruff the third diamond and lead a trump, which East will duck. Then, you won't be able to cash a diamond, because West still has a trump, and you won't be able to ruff a spade, because either defender is in a position to draw dummy's remaining trump.

Alternatively, you might win with the ace of clubs and play three high diamonds from dummy, discarding two clubs. West will ruff and now ace and another heart will leave you with two spade losers.

The best play is not easy to see. Cash just two diamonds, the ace and queen, throwing one club and then duck a spade. The defenders can cash one club and must stand every chance of making the ace of trumps, but that will be all.

Stout Fellow

♠ A Q 2
♡ 3
◇ A 4 3
♣ K 9 8 5 4 2

```
        N
  W         E
        S
```

♠J led

♠ K 5 3
♡ A J 8 5
◇ K 7 5 2
♣ A 3

Dealer North
N–S vul.

WEST	NORTH	EAST	SOUTH
	1♣	pass	1♡
pass	2♣	pass	3NT
all pass			

Most of the time it pays to concentrate on looking for fits in the major suits. When partner opens 1♣, the only two likely contracts with this hand are 4♡ and 3NT, so you do not bother responding 'up the line' with 1◇ to look for a diamond fit. Of course, on a bad day partner would hold ♠A2 ♡3 ◇AQ43 ♣K98542 when even the grand slam in diamonds is a fair contract.

After a spade lead you will have plenty of tricks if the clubs break 3-2, but of course they may not. Even if they divide 4-1 you should come to enough tricks, always assuming that the defenders don't take five tricks before you have landed nine (or ten). What is your first move?

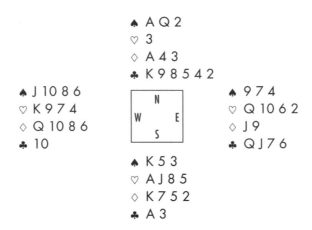

                    ♠ A Q 2
                    ♡ 3
                    ◇ A 4 3
                    ♣ K 9 8 5 4 2
♠ J 10 8 6   ♠ 9 7 4
♡ K 9 7 4   N   ♡ Q 10 6 2
◇ Q 10 8 6   W   E   ◇ J 9
♣ 10   S   ♣ Q J 7 6
                    ♠ K 5 3
                    ♡ A J 8 5
                    ◇ K 7 5 2
                    ♣ A 3

You play in 3NT and West leads the jack of spades.

There will be plenty of tricks if the clubs break 3-2 or if East
has a high singleton, so it may seem tempting to win the spade
lead with the king and immediately lay down the ace of clubs.
The disadvantage of this play comes if East has the double guard,
as he will be able to lead hearts twice from his side.

If you have noted the value of the eight of hearts, then you
will appreciate that one lead of the suit from the West hand, and
one from East, will not prove fatal to your cause.

Win the spade lead in dummy, therefore, and lead a small
club. When East plays low, do the same. West will win with his
singleton ten and will probably lead a heart to the queen and ace.
You cash the ace of clubs, cross to dummy and play king and
another club. East will try the ten of hearts now (he hopes that
West began with K-9-8-x); you cover with the jack, and the eight
will protect you from further assault.

Note that your heart suit would still constitute a double stopper even if East were able to lead the suit first. You would simply cover whatever card he led.

Success for Plan B

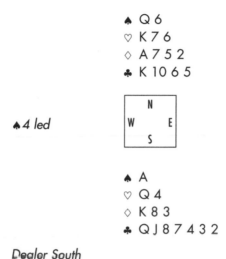

♠ Q 6
♡ K 7 6
◇ A 7 5 2
♣ K 10 6 5

♠4 led

♠ A
♡ Q 4
◇ K 8 3
♣ Q J 8 7 4 3 2

Dealer South
E–W vul.

WEST	NORTH	EAST	SOUTH
			1♣
2♣¹	2♡²	3♠	5♣
all pass			

1. Michaels, at least 5-5 in the majors.
2. Club support and a heart stopper.

You have avoided 3NT, which would have had no play on a spade lead. How, though, can you make five clubs on the same lead? It seems there are three losers — two aces and a diamond.

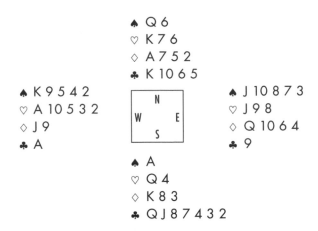

```
              ♠ Q 6
              ♡ K 7 6
              ◇ A 7 5 2
              ♣ K 10 6 5
♠ K 9 5 4 2    ┌─────────┐    ♠ J 10 8 7 3
♡ A 10 5 3 2   │    N    │    ♡ J 9 8
◇ J 9          │ W     E │    ◇ Q 10 6 4
♣ A            │    S    │    ♣ 9
               └─────────┘
              ♠ A
              ♡ Q 4
              ◇ K 8 3
              ♣ Q J 8 7 4 3 2
```

Defending against 5♣, West reasonably leads a spade rather than a heart.

You can see three possible — indeed, probable — losers. A good plan would be to put up the queen of spades from dummy. If the king and ace head this, next you can play a small heart from hand. This might look like a singleton and West might fly in with the ace hoping to cash a spade. Then you would have a discard for your losing diamond.

This vision disappears when East cannot cover the queen of spades and you have to overtake with the ace. Have you any reserve play in mind?

You might try this: cash the king and ace of diamonds, ruff a spade, and exit with a club. As the cards lie, this forces West to give you a ruff and discard or lead a heart, which will run to the queen. Then a heart from hand will set up a discard. We reckon this is the line to go for.

We would like to remark that West could have avoided this untimely throw-in if he had begun with the ace of clubs. The singleton ace of trumps is often a dangerous card to retain.

♠ 7 3
♡ A Q 7
◇ K Q J 6
♣ A Q 7 3

♣J led

♠ K Q J 8 5 4 2
♡ —
◇ A 9 3 2
♣ K 8

Dealer South
Both vul.

WEST	NORTH	EAST	SOUTH
			1♠
pass	2◇	pass	4♠
pass	6♠	all pass	

Agreed, the players here have not conducted a particularly scientific auction, but sometimes it pays not to paint too accurate a picture. These days North would probably use Roman Keycard Blackwood at his second turn, as South's response would rarely benefit the defending side.

The contract looks fairly safe, but how you do intend to play after West's club lead? Remember, if normal breaks present no difficulty, you should seek to cater for an unfriendly layout.

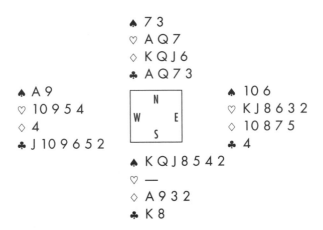

```
              ♠ 7 3
              ♡ A Q 7
              ◇ K Q J 6
              ♣ A Q 7 3
  ♠ A 9           N          ♠ 10 6
  ♡ 10 9 5 4                 ♡ K J 8 6 3 2
  ◇ 4        W        E      ◇ 10 8 7 5
  ♣ J 10 9 6 5 2    S        ♣ 4
              ♠ K Q J 8 5 4 2
              ♡ —
              ◇ A 9 3 2
              ♣ K 8
```

After an auction that gives little away, you reach 6♠, and West leads the jack of clubs.

Did you, by any chance, spend your time calculating the possibility of a trump reduction that might see you home if East turned up with ♠A-10-9-x? You must have found it a bit frustrating; dummy contains too few entries unless East holds diamond length as well. (After taking the club with the queen, ruffing a heart to hand and laying down a top spade, you would need the ◇K-Q-J all to serve as entries. Then you could take two more ruffs, lead one trump through East, forcing him to split the 10-9, and get back to dummy at the finish.)

In any case, a 6-1 break in clubs, with the ace of trumps in the hand containing the long clubs, seems more likely. So forget about the trump reduction. Win the first trick with the queen of clubs and hurriedly dispose of the club king on the ace of hearts. Now, when you play a trump to the king and it loses to the ace, you can overruff East on the second round of clubs. If East were the one with long clubs and the trump ace, you would still be all right. He would have to play his ace on a small card, so you could afford to ruff the club high.

Take a Hint

♠ A 7 5
♡ Q J
♢ Q 8 5
♣ K Q 8 7 3

```
        N
  W          E
        S
```

♡ 4 led

♠ K 10 4 2
♡ K 8
♢ A 6 3
♣ A 10 4 2

Dealer South
E–W vul.

WEST	NORTH	EAST	SOUTH
			1NT¹
pass	3NT	all pass	

1. 12-14

Having the same doubleton in each hand often spells the death of a 3NT contract, at any rate if an opponent leads the suit. Thankfully, you have reserves of values: 28 points rather than the usual minimum of 25. Will they be enough?

West leads the four of hearts and East follows with the six. As West would surely lead the ten from ♡A-10-9-4 and East would hardly play the six from ♡10-9-7-6, a blockage in the heart suit sounds improbable and you will need to take nine tricks rather smartly. After winning this trick, what is your first move?

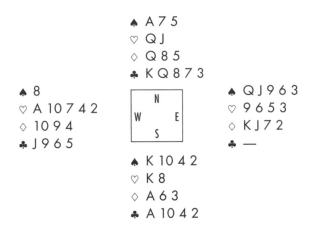

```
                    ♠ A 7 5
                    ♡ Q J
                    ◇ Q 8 5
                    ♣ K Q 8 7 3
♠ 8                                    ♠ Q J 9 6 3
♡ A 10 7 4 2          N                ♡ 9 6 5 3
◇ 10 9 4          W       E            ◇ K J 7 2
♣ J 9 6 5             S                ♣ —
                    ♠ K 10 4 2
                    ♡ K 8
                    ◇ A 6 3
                    ♣ A 10 4 2
```

You play in 3NT and West leads the four of hearts, on which East plays an encouraging six.

You can make this contract easily if the clubs yield five tricks, and you can ensure this even against a 4-0 break on either side so long as you begin with the 'right' high card. Since West figures to hold longer hearts than his partner (the two and three are both missing), you may feel inclined to begin with the king of clubs — but don't act too hastily! For one thing, the opening leader often has more cards in the suit he chooses to lead against a notrump contract than does his partner, so you cannot attach too much weight to this information. Besides, there may be indications if you test the other suits first.

The only suit you can test, as it happens, is spades. You can lay down the ace and king, anyway. You find that East has five spades, while West discards the four of diamonds.

You are the sort of person to take a hint. With the spades 5-1 and East presumably holding at least four hearts, you would expect him, if anyone, to be short in clubs. Change your mind and begin with the ace. When East shows out on this trick you have a marked double finesse, with the ace of diamonds as your re-entry for leading clubs from hand again.

Pretty as a Picture

♠ 9 5 3
♡ K Q 6
◇ K Q 7 3
♣ K Q 10

♠4 led

♠ A
♡ A 10 4 2
◇ 6 5 4
♣ A J 9 8 2

Dealer South
Both vul.

WEST	NORTH	EAST	SOUTH
			1♣
pass	1◇	pass	1♡
pass	2♠ *	pass	3♣
pass	4♣	pass	4NT
pass	5◇	pass	6♣
all pass			

Both players have done a little too much bidding, perhaps. At any rate, the contract of 6♣ seems on the optimistic side, because you will need to find the ace of diamonds well placed, and that may not be the end of the affair.

The first trick goes to the king and ace of spades and all follow when you draw two rounds of trumps with the king and jack. What do you do next?

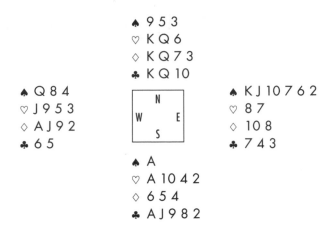

♠ 9 5 3
♡ K Q 6
◇ K Q 7 3
♣ K Q 10

♠ Q 8 4
♡ J 9 5 3
◇ A J 9 2
♣ 6 5

N
W E
S

♠ K J 10 7 6 2
♡ 8 7
◇ 10 8
♣ 7 4 3

♠ A
♡ A 10 4 2
◇ 6 5 4
♣ A J 9 8 2

You play in 6♣; West leads a spade to the king and ace.

After two rounds of trumps, play a diamond to the king. Then draw the last trump with the ♣A (better than playing on hearts) and lead another diamond. If West ducks (best), the position is:

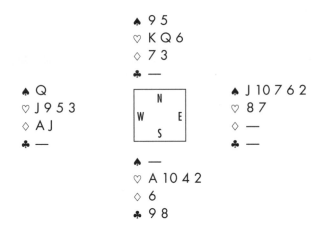

♠ 9 5
♡ K Q 6
◇ 7 3
♣ —

♠ Q
♡ J 9 5 3
◇ A J
♣ —

N
W E
S

♠ J 10 7 6 2
♡ 8 7
◇ —
♣ —

♠ —
♡ A 10 4 2
◇ 6
♣ 9 8

Now you lead a spade from dummy and pitch a diamond. West wins and leads a diamond, so you ruff and play your last trump. If East won the spade, you could ruff a spade exit and then West could not keep four hearts and two diamonds.

Lonely Heart

```
        ♠ 7 4
        ♡ A K Q 6 5 4
        ◇ 9 7 5
        ♣ 9 4
```

```
              ┌─────────┐
              │    N    │
◇ 6 led       │ W     E │
              │    S    │
              └─────────┘
```

```
        ♠ A K 9 2
        ♡ 10 2
        ◇ A J 3
        ♣ A J 8 5
```

Dealer North
N–S vul.

WEST	NORTH	EAST	SOUTH
	2♡	pass	2NT
pass	3NT	all pass	

Your 2NT response to the weak two inquires about the strength of North's hand and the quality of his suit. The 3NT rebid conveys a special message: the ♡A-K-Q and, by inference, extremely little outside (or he would have opened 1♡).

West leads the ◇6 and East contributes the king. The first question is how you will play on the first two tricks; the second is how will you tackle the hearts.

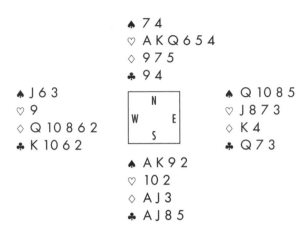

                ♠ 7 4
                ♡ A K Q 6 5 4
                ◊ 9 7 5
                ♣ 9 4

    ♠ J 6 3   ♠ Q 10 8 5
    ♡ 9   N   ♡ J 8 7 3
    ◊ Q 10 8 6 2   W   E   ◊ K 4
    ♣ K 10 6 2   S   ♣ Q 7 3

                ♠ A K 9 2
                ♡ 10 2
                ◊ A J 3
                ♣ A J 8 5

You are in 3NT and West leads a small diamond to the king.

Usually you win with the ace when holding A-J-x because this will give you a further stopper if West gains the lead. Here, though, you plan to attack hearts and East stands more chance of gaining the lead (if someone has J-x-x-x of hearts, it is probably the defender short in diamonds). You must also bear in mind that if you duck too many rounds of diamonds, then you might lose two tricks in each minor as well as a heart.

Therefore, win the second round of diamonds and advance the ♡10. If West covers with the jack, you will have to win in dummy and play for six heart tricks; otherwise, duck in dummy, ensuring five tricks, which are all you need. You will rarely lose this contract unless West turns up with a singleton ♡J.

This layout is similar:

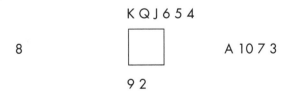

              K Q J 6 5 4

    8   A 10 7 3

              9 2

Let's assume dummy has one outside entry and you can afford to lose two tricks. If West is the danger hand, you should run the nine.

King's Counsel

♠ K 8 4 2
♡ K
◇ A 9 5
♣ A Q J 9 7

♣ 10 led

♠ 3
♡ A 8
◇ Q J 10 8 7 3
♣ 6 4 3 2

Dealer North
Both vul.

WEST	NORTH	EAST	SOUTH
	1♣	pass	1◇
1♠	2NT	pass	3♣
pass	3◇	pass	4◇
pass	5◇	all pass	

You may not approve of North's 2NT, but the sequence arose at rubber bridge when a double of 1♠ would mean penalties.

West's lead of the ♣10 *might* be a tricky play from K-10, but you shouldn't assume this unless no other chance exists. The entry situation looks awkward and you have to work out how to avoid three losers.

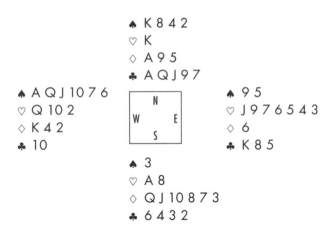

```
                        ♠ K 8 4 2
                        ♡ K
                        ◊ A 9 5
                        ♣ A Q J 9 7
    ♠ A Q J 10 7 6   ┌─────────┐      ♠ 9 5
    ♡ Q 10 2         │    N    │      ♡ J 9 7 6 5 4 3
    ◊ K 4 2          │ W     E │      ◊ 6
    ♣ 10             │    S    │      ♣ K 8 5
                     └─────────┘
                        ♠ 3
                        ♡ A 8
                        ◊ Q J 10 8 7 3
                        ♣ 6 4 3 2
```

You play in 5◊ and West, who has overcalled in spades, leads the ten of clubs through a suit bid by dummy.

As you don't want to lose a club ruff and go down even with the trump finesse right, you put up the ace of clubs. You may think now of coming to hand by overtaking the king of hearts with the ace. The snag in this play is that if you need to draw three rounds of diamonds to pick up the king, you will have a heart to lose when East takes the king of clubs. This danger seems very real (a) because West would think twice about trying for a ruff without K-x-x of trumps and (b) if he held at least four cards in each major then he might well have made a takeout double; his likely shape is 6-3-3-1.

You want to gain entry to hand without setting up a winner for the opposition or allowing East into the lead. Well, the king of spades is not going to play an important part later in the play, is it? Begin your campaign by leading this card and you will soon be able to enter hand with a spade ruff, pick up the diamond king, and lose just one spade and one club. If West has led from ♣K-10 doubleton (or K-10-x) and the trump finesse loses then you will have to take your hat off to him.

March Past

```
              ♠ A 8 6 5
              ♡ K J 7 3
              ◊ A J 8 5
              ♣ 7

              ┌─────────┐
              │    N    │
  ♣ 3 led     │ W     E │
              │    S    │
              └─────────┘

              ♠ K Q 3 2
              ♡ A 8 6 4
              ◊ 10
              ♣ A K J 5
```

Dealer North
Neither vul.

WEST	NORTH	EAST	SOUTH
	1◊	pass	1♡
pass	2♡	pass	2♠
pass	4♡	pass	6♡
all pass			

With four trumps and a singleton, North is right to decline to sign off in 3♡ but, as he anticipates being dummy, he should make a more descriptive bid than 4♡. He could bid 4♣, to show the club singleton, or 3♠ to indicate spade support.

West leads the ♣3 to the ten and jack. There are many possible lines of play. We advise the simplest — begin with ace and king of hearts. You have not done so well, because this leaves West with the Q-10. Can you see any chance now?

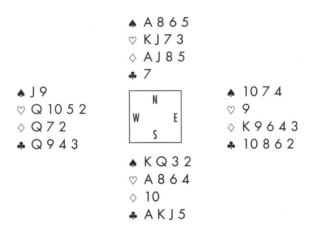

You are in 6♡; West leads a club to the ten and jack.

You begin with the ♡A and ♡K, and if all follow, you will have no problem. When the bad news comes, cash the ♠A-K and then pitch two spades from dummy on the ♣A-K. This leaves:

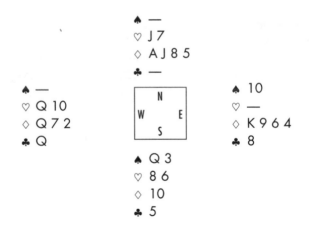

Now lead the ♠Q, which West does best not to ruff. Then you can ruff a club, play ace and ruff a diamond, and you finish in hand for a delightful *coup-en-passant* — whether West ruffs the last spade high or low, dummy's ♡J will get to score.

Immediate Offer

```
              ♠ Q 10 7
              ♡ K Q 10 6 3
              ◇ A
              ♣ 9 6 4 2

              ┌─────────┐
              │    N    │
◇ 6 led       │ W     E │
              │    S    │
              └─────────┘

              ♠ A K J
              ♡ 5 2
              ◇ K 9 8 5 2
              ♣ A 10 5
```

Dealer South
N–S vul.

WEST	NORTH	EAST	SOUTH
			1NT
pass	2◇	pass	2♡
pass	3NT	all pass	

Modern players happily open a 15-17 1NT even with a small doubleton, since it enables them to convey the nature of their hand. Here you had no choice, because in your system, after 1◇-1♡, a rebid of 1NT would imply a weaker hand, one not good enough for a 1NT opening. You might, of course, open 1◇ and rebid 1♠ — but that misdescribes the shape.

The sequence turns out fairly well here when West leads your five-card suit. Even so, with the duplication in spades and an awkward entry situation, a struggle looms.

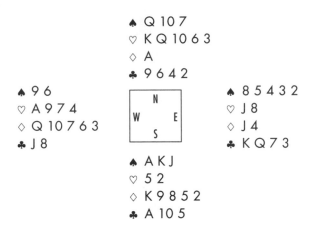

♠ Q 10 7
♡ K Q 10 6 3
◇ A
♣ 9 6 4 2

♠ 9 6
♡ A 9 7 4
◇ Q 10 7 6 3
♣ J 8

♠ 8 5 4 3 2
♡ J 8
◇ J 4
♣ K Q 7 3

♠ A K J
♡ 5 2
◇ K 9 8 5 2
♣ A 10 5

You play in 3NT and West leads the six of diamonds to dummy's ace.

With only six top tricks, you will surely need to develop the hearts, and you can probably afford to lose two tricks in the suit. (On the first trick, you should drop the five of diamonds from hand, making it more likely that the defenders will pursue the diamonds when they get in again and not switch to clubs.)

With a combination like A-Q-x-x-x opposite x-x, players are fully accustomed to ducking the first round, but with the present heart layout the idea generally fails to occur to them. Having only one more entry to dummy, you should lead a small heart from dummy after winning the diamond. Three heart tricks will always be possible if the suit breaks 3-3 and against many other combinations, for example A-x or A-x-x-x in the West hand.

Here East may or may not go in with the jack. Whether he does or not, the defenders are likely to continue diamonds. You grab the king and pursue the hearts, playing to the king next, and easily score the nine tricks. You would still be all right if East switched to a small club. Trusting that he has not led small from K-Q-J-x, you would go up with the ace and block the suit.

Best of Three

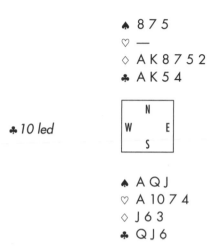

```
        ♠ 8 7 5
        ♡ —
        ◇ A K 8 7 5 2
        ♣ A K 5 4

             N
♣ 10 led   W     E
             S

        ♠ A Q J
        ♡ A 10 7 4
        ◇ J 6 3
        ♣ Q J 6
```

Dealer South
Both vul.

WEST	NORTH	EAST	SOUTH
			1NT¹
pass	2NT	pass	3◇
pass	4♣	pass	4◇
pass	4♡	pass	4♠
pass	6◇	all pass	

After your strong notrump, North's 2NT was a transfer, showing
a diamond suit. If you had A-x-x or K-x-x of diamonds, you
would have broken the transfer by bidding 3♣. Your actual 3◇
denied such a holding — not that this was news to North. The
next two bids, 4♣ and 4◇, were natural and the two after that
cuebids.

West leads the ten of clubs against six diamonds. The hands
do not fit well; the ace of hearts seems to pull little weight. How
will you set about the play?

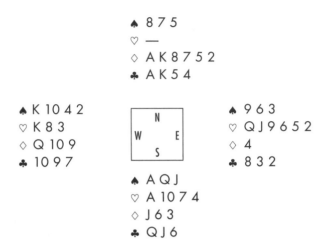

♠ 8 7 5
♡ —
◇ A K 8 7 5 2
♣ A K 5 4

♠ K 10 4 2
♡ K 8 3
◇ Q 10 9
♣ 10 9 7

♠ 9 6 3
♡ Q J 9 6 5 2
◇ 4
♣ 8 3 2

♠ A Q J
♡ A 10 7 4
◇ J 6 3
♣ Q J 6

After you opened 1NT, you wind up in 6◇, and West leads the ten of clubs.

Your first thought may be that to make your slam you need to either bring down the queen of diamonds or find East with the king of spades; both appear quite good chances. Another idea is to win the club lead in dummy and take an early spade finesse. If this wins, you can afford a safety play in trumps — low from dummy so that you can pick up ◇Q-10-9-x on either side.

Slightly better is to consider the possibility of finding West with ◇Q-10-x or ◇Q-9-x, the king of spades and not more than three hearts. Win the club in hand, ruff a heart and cash the ◇A-K. Then you cross back with a club and play ace and another heart, ruffing. Now cash another club and, when all follow, exit with a trump. As the cards lie, this forces West to lead a spade.

'If only you had been on lead, we beat it,' West may remark. 'I could have doubled four spades and you would have known what to do.'

'Yes, perhaps we should take up these four-suit transfers,' East replies.

Finally, did you spot that you might bring off the endplay even if West holds four hearts? If he has a 2–4–3–4 shape, you can ruff the fourth club in hand and ruff another heart.

finesse not Wanted

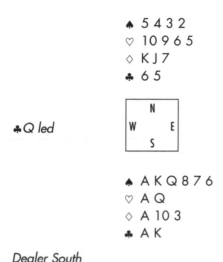

                    ♠ 5 4 3 2
                    ♡ 10 9 6 5
                    ◇ K J 7
                    ♣ 6 5

♣Q led

                    ♠ A K Q 8 7 6
                    ♡ A Q
                    ◇ A 10 3
                    ♣ A K

Dealer South
Both vul.

WEST	NORTH	EAST	SOUTH
			2♣
pass	2◇	pass	2♠
pass	3♠	pass	4♣
pass	4◇	pass	4♡
pass	4♠	pass	6♠
all pass			

Many players now use 'Italian style' or 'Multi' cuebids, showing first- and second-round controls indiscriminately at the three-level and four-level, knowing 4NT is available to check on aces. Even using traditional 'first-round controls first', North can bid 4◇ as you know he holds a weak hand.

West leads the ♣Q and dummy puts down the minimum expected. How will you plan to make four tricks in the red suits?

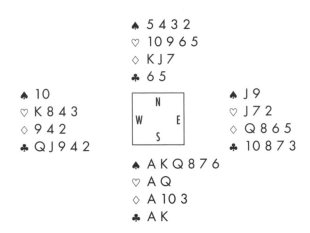

```
              ♠ 5 4 3 2
              ♡ 10 9 6 5
              ◇ K J 7
              ♣ 6 5
♠ 10                            ♠ J 9
♡ K 8 4 3      N                ♡ J 7 2
◇ 9 4 2      W   E              ◇ Q 8 6 5
♣ Q J 9 4 2    S                ♣ 10 8 7 3
              ♠ A K Q 8 7 6
              ♡ A Q
              ◇ A 10 3
              ♣ A K
```

You play in 6♠ and West leads the club queen.

You have excellent prospects, obviously. If, after drawing trumps, you play ace and another diamond, finessing the jack, you will still have the heart finesse in reserve. You are about 3:1 on to win one of the two finesses, with the small extra chance of a singleton queen of diamonds in the East hand.

However, you can do quite a bit better by drawing trumps, cashing the second club, and playing ace and queen of hearts from hand.

You are home now if West has the king of hearts, because when he comes in with this card he will be on play, forced to lead a heart through dummy's 10-9 or a diamond.

You will also win if East has the king of hearts whenever West produces a singleton, doubleton or tripleton jack of hearts or East has K-J-x — in the last two cases East will exit with a heart and you will ruff to bring down the jack. Finally, if East has a doubleton ♡K-x, he will be endplayed.

At worst, East may hold ♡K-J-x-x-x or ♡K-J-x-x or ♡K-x-x but, even then, you still have the diamond finesse in reserve. (Yes, you might try for a squeeze instead.)

Invitation to the Dance

```
        ♠ A Q J 6
        ♡ A K
        ◇ 10 7 3
        ♣ J 9 6 4
```

```
              ┌─────┐
              │  N  │
  ◇ 5 led     │W   E│
              │  S  │
              └─────┘
```

```
        ♠ 10 9 7 3 2
        ♡ Q 7
        ◇ Q 4 2
        ♣ A Q 10
```

Dealer East
Neither vul.

WEST	NORTH	EAST	SOUTH
		pass	pass
pass	1♣	pass	1♠
pass	3♠	pass	4♠
all pass			

A 1NT opening by North here would have been weak; hence the 1♣ opening.

West leads a small diamond and East plays king, ace and another, your queen winning the third round. The diamond position has turned out nicely, though you still cannot afford to find both black kings on the wrong side. Perhaps you see a plan that might help you to succeed even if they are?

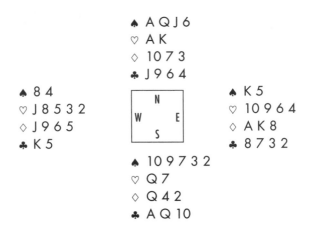

                    ♠ A Q J 6
                    ♡ A K
                    ◇ 10 7 3
                    ♣ J 9 6 4

♠ 8 4   ♠ K 5
♡ J 8 5 3 2   ♡ 10 9 6 4
◇ J 9 6 5   ◇ A K 8
♣ K 5   ♣ 8 7 3 2

                    ♠ 10 9 7 3 2
                    ♡ Q 7
                    ◇ Q 4 2
                    ♣ A Q 10

After North has opened 1♣ in fourth position, you play in 4♠. West leads a small diamond and East plays ace, king and another, you winning with the queen.

The simple game is to take two finesses, one in spades and one in clubs. You should reflect, however, that if the king of spades sits over the ace, the king of clubs will do so too, since East passed as dealer.

Against strong opposition, particularly, it would be clever play to lay down the ace of clubs. If you are wasting a trick, it will not matter, because in that case the spade finesse will surely work. What may happen is that West, wondering why you are leading the ace of clubs at this early stage, may place you with A-x-x and unblock the king — he doesn't want to have to give you a ruff and discard.

What happens if all play low on the ace of clubs? Then finesse in trumps, because if the finesse loses you were going down anyway.

Finally, did you spot a way for West to avoid facing the dilemma? If he had dropped the jack on the second round of diamonds, East would have known you had the ◇Q and shifted to the seven or eight of clubs, denying strength in the suit.

Pin Money

```
            ♠ A J
            ♡ A K 3
            ◇ K 9 7 3
            ♣ J 7 5 4
```

```
                  ┌──────────┐
                  │    N     │
  ♠ 2 led         │ W      E │
                  │    S     │
                  └──────────┘
```

```
            ♠ K 5
            ♡ 10 8 6 5 2
            ◇ A Q J 4
            ♣ A Q
```

Dealer West
N–S vul.

WEST	NORTH	EAST	SOUTH
pass	1NT	pass	3♡
pass	3♠	pass	4♣
pass	4♡	pass	6♡
all pass			

The simple systems permitted at the rubber bridge table (no transfers, for example) tend to make it difficult to bid slams accurately even when the players are experts. Six diamonds would have been a slightly better contract, but it is too late to think about that now.

In 6♡, you will need to escape ill fortune in hearts and clubs. How will you begin the play and how will you continue?

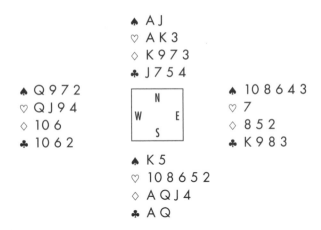

♠ A J
♥ A K 3
♦ K 9 7 3
♣ J 7 5 4

♠ Q 9 7 2
♥ Q J 9 4
♦ 10 6
♣ 10 6 2

♠ 10 8 6 4 3
♥ 7
♦ 8 5 2
♣ K 9 8 3

♠ K 5
♥ 10 8 6 5 2
♦ A Q J 4
♣ A Q

You play in 6♥ after North has opened a strong notrump. West leads the two of spades.

You have a likely loser in hearts and a 50-50 chance of a loser in clubs. Since you could play the hearts in a number of ways and the risk of an adverse ruff appears minimal, it is right to go up with the ace of spades and test the clubs first. To your surprise, the queen of clubs holds.

Now you must aim to lose at most one trick in hearts. If the suit divides 3-2, you can't go wrong. So suppose it breaks 4-1. You can give yourself an extra chance by an almost unknown safety play: lead the eight and let it run if West plays low.

It may have occurred to you that leading the ten of hearts on the first round would pin either a singleton seven or singleton nine. However, it wouldn't work so well if West held a singleton jack or queen; in that case leading the eight still wins.

What a terror this position is! If West plays the jack or queen on your lead of the eight, you must not bang out the ace and king; you must come back via the ♠K and lead the ♥6 (or ♥10).

Take a bonus point if you spotted but rejected an endplay for when West has three hearts and the king of clubs. Unless he is very short in spades, it would not work.

Dubious Convention

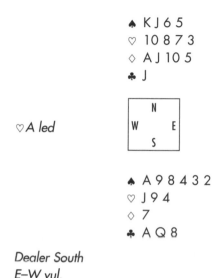

♠ K J 6 5
♡ 10 8 7 3
◇ A J 10 5
♣ J

♡ A led

```
      N
  W       E
      S
```

♠ A 9 8 4 3 2
♡ J 9 4
◇ 7
♣ A Q 8

Dealer South
E–W vul.

WEST	NORTH	EAST	SOUTH
			1♠
2NT	4♠	all pass	

West's 2NT, denoting a minor two-suiter, is a double-edged sword. If the side that makes a two-suited bid manages to buy the contract, or if it helps them push their opponents into the wrong spot, it tends to show a profit. By contrast, if neither condition applies, it provides declarer with a blueprint of the distribution. Here it seems that West has been unlucky as East appears to hold a much weaker hand than North.

Against 4♠, West cashes the ace and king of hearts (not necessarily denying A-K doubleton), and then leads the king of diamonds to dummy's ace. How should you proceed?

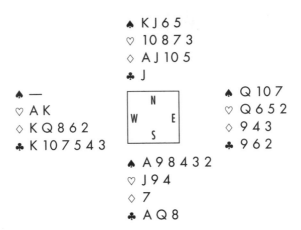

♠ K J 6 5
♡ 10 8 7 3
◇ A J 10 5
♣ J

♠ —
♡ A K
◇ K Q 8 6 2
♣ K 10 7 5 4 3

♠ Q 10 7
♡ Q 6 5 2
◇ 9 4 3
♣ 9 6 2

♠ A 9 8 4 3 2
♡ J 9 4
◇ 7
♣ A Q 8

You play in 4♠ after West has overcalled with an 'unusual' 2NT, denoting a minor two-suiter. West cashes the ace and king of hearts, then leads the king of diamonds.

It seems quite likely that the spades will split 3-0, in which case the only chance is to endplay East. You should crossruff diamonds and clubs, arriving at this position:

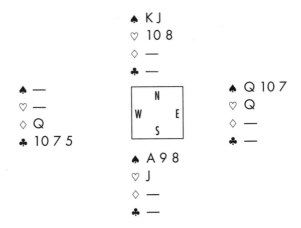

♠ K J
♡ 10 8
◇ —
♣ —

♠ —
♡ —
◇ Q
♣ 10 7 5

♠ Q 10 7
♡ Q
◇ —
♣ —

♠ A 9 8
♡ J
◇ —
♣ —

A heart exit leaves East only able to wave the white flag.

The Long and the Short

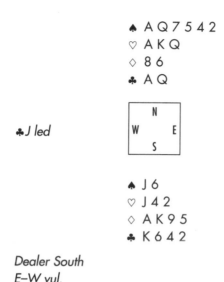

♠ A Q 7 5 4 2
♡ A K Q
◇ 8 6
♣ A Q

♣J led

          N
      W   E
          S

♠ J 6
♡ J 4 2
◇ A K 9 5
♣ K 6 4 2

Dealer South
E–W vul.

WEST	NORTH	EAST	SOUTH
			1NT[1]
pass	6NT	all pass	

1. 12-14

In an IMP pairs event those playing a weak notrump had the opportunity to take a short route to slam, whilst some pairs toiled away for five or six rounds of bidding to arrive at the same contract. With the queen in his three-card suit, North could see that it was impossible for your hand to contain a useful ruffing value, so he didn't bother to look for a spade fit.

West leads the jack of clubs and prospects seem good. Indeed a 3-2 spade break would make the slam laydown. How will you set about the play?

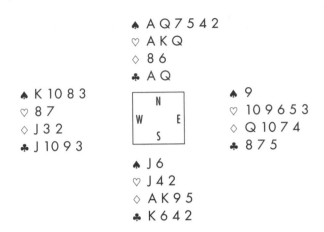

♠ A Q 7 5 4 2
♥ A K Q
♦ 8 6
♣ A Q

♠ K 10 8 3   ♠ 9
♥ 8 7   ♥ 10 9 6 5 3
♦ J 3 2   ♦ Q 10 7 4
♣ J 10 9 3   ♣ 8 7 5

♠ J 6
♥ J 4 2
♦ A K 9 5
♣ K 6 4 2

You play in 6NT, the best contract on the deal, and West leads the jack of clubs.

As they say, one should always form a plan before playing to the first trick. Some players, in a pairs event that used teams scoring, won with the queen of clubs and then played ace and another spade, remarking afterwards that at least they had made a safety play in spades. Leading the ace of course wins against a singleton king on either side and is *generally* the right play with A-Q-x-x-x-x opposite J-x. Here, however, the presence of the seven, six and five tilts the odds towards leading the jack from hand. Then declarer can score five tricks in spades when East turns up with a singleton eight, nine or ten.

Not so easy to see in time is that entries may present a problem if you win with the ace of clubs, come to hand with the diamond ace and lead the jack of spades. West covers and the ace brings down the nine. Now you cannot conveniently enter hand with either minor-suit king and you will be setting up at least a second winner for the defenders if you try to.

The answer is that at Trick 1 you should overtake the ♣Q with the ♣K, and then follow with the ♠J. After heading the king with the ace, you cross to the ♦K for the next spade lead.

Delicate Approach

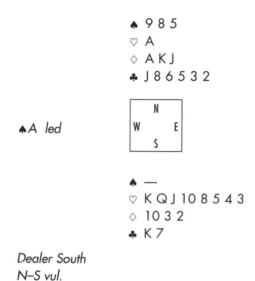

♠ 9 8 5
♡ A
◇ A K J
♣ J 8 6 5 3 2

♠A led

♠ —
♡ K Q J 10 8 5 4 3
◇ 10 3 2
♣ K 7

Dealer South
N–S vul.

WEST	NORTH	EAST	SOUTH
			4♡
4♠	5♡	all pass	

We would not fault North for doubling 4♠, but he prefers to try
for the vulnerable game instead. If, as seems to happen with sur-
prising frequency, the 4♡ opening includes a void in spades, then
the hands will fit well.

West leads the ♠A and you ruff. You don't want to lose two
clubs and a diamond. How can you make the most of your
chances?

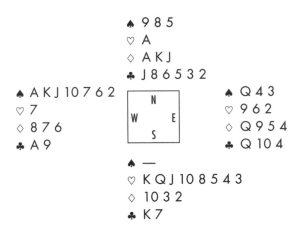

```
                    ♠ 9 8 5
                    ♡ A
                    ◇ A K J
                    ♣ J 8 6 5 3 2
♠ A K J 10 7 6 2   ┌─────────┐    ♠ Q 4 3
♡ 7                │    N    │    ♡ 9 6 2
◇ 8 7 6            │ W     E │    ◇ Q 9 5 4
♣ A 9              │    S    │    ♣ Q 10 4
                   └─────────┘
                    ♠ —
                    ♡ K Q J 10 8 5 4 3
                    ◇ 10 3 2
                    ♣ K 7
```

You play in 5♡ after West has made an overcall of 4♠. West leads the ace of spades. East plays the three, and you ruff.

You would like to establish a trick in clubs so that you won't need to take the diamond finesse, but entry problems loom. If you cross to the ace of hearts to lead a club to the king, West might win and lead a diamond. This will leave you unable to do anything with the clubs.

It is sensible, therefore, to begin by leading a small club from hand. If West plays the ace or queen, you will surely come to a club trick. As the cards lie, West's nine is covered by the jack and queen. East will probably return a trump. Now you can play a second round of clubs and all will go smoothly, since you have protected dummy's diamond entries.

This line ensures success unless East holds ♣A-Q-10-9 and the ◇Q. In that case he might have taken some action over five hearts and West might have led his singleton club. In any event, you can still succeed via a trump squeeze if you pick up the vibes that the diamond finesse is not working.

North did well, as you see, to bid 5♡. With the club suit frozen, 4♠ doubled would have made.

Pretty Boy

```
            ♠ 10
            ♡ A J 5
            ◇ A K 7 6 3
            ♣ Q 8 4 2
```

```
                    ┌─────────┐
                    │    N    │
    ♡ Q led         │ W     E │
                    │    S    │
                    └─────────┘
```

```
            ♠ A K Q J 8 4 2
            ♡ 9 4 3
            ◇ 10 2
            ♣ 6
```

Dealer West
N–S vul.

WEST	NORTH	EAST	SOUTH
pass	1◇	1♡	4♠
all pass			

You should probably have taken the auction more slowly: if North had ♡K-x-x or ♡Q-J-x, 3NT might easily have been a superior contract. We guess that the lure of being able to claim 100 points above the line for holding four of the top five trumps proved too hard to resist.

West leads the queen of hearts and you have visions of a big rubber. This may look like a silly problem but we can assure you that it isn't.

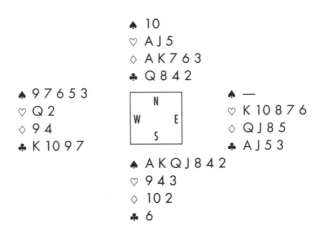

```
                    ♠ 10
                    ♡ A J 5
                    ◇ A K 7 6 3
                    ♣ Q 8 4 2
   ♠ 9 7 6 5 3                        ♠ —
   ♡ Q 2          ┌─────────┐        ♡ K 10 8 7 6
   ◇ 9 4          │   N     │        ◇ Q J 8 5
   ♣ K 10 9 7     │ W     E │        ♣ A J 5 3
                  │   S     │
                  └─────────┘
                    ♠ A K Q J 8 4 2
                    ♡ 9 4 3
                    ◇ 10 2
                    ♣ 6
```

You play in 4♠ after North has opened 1◇ and East has overcalled 1♡. West leads the queen of hearts.

Oh good! You see ten tricks on top and mentally start adding
up the rubber. You take dummy's ♡A — no point in holding off
— and lead the ten of spades. East shows out and suddenly trouble looms, because you lack a quick entry to hand. You may try
ace, king and another diamond, but West overruffs and the vision
of a big rubber has disappeared.

It looked too easy and you neglected to make a play that you
have seen in many problems. To ensure that you will be able to
go from hand to hand whenever you want, begin by playing a
club from dummy, ideally the queen. The best that East can do
is let West win the club, then score two hearts, and perhaps lead
another heart. Now you can ruff low and, if West overruffs, you
still have the pretty ten of spades in dummy.

You could count yourself unlucky if giving up a club early
costs the contract. Surely, this would only happen if East holds
5-5 in the reds, in which case West could discard his singleton
diamond on the third round of hearts and then obtain a ruff. The
actual layout seems rather more likely.

On Your Side

```
        ♠ A Q 5 4
        ♡ 9 6
        ◇ K 8
        ♣ K 10 7 4 2

             ┌─────────┐
             │    N    │
♠ 10 led     │ W     E │
             │    S    │
             └─────────┘

        ♠ K J 3
        ♡ K 10 8
        ◇ A Q J 10
        ♣ A Q 5
```

Dealer South
Both vul.

WEST	NORTH	EAST	SOUTH
			2NT
pass	3♣*	pass	3◇
pass	3♠	pass	3NT
pass	6NT	all pass	

North's 3♣ is not Stayman but Baron, asking for four-card suits up the line. When no fit comes to light, he quite reasonably takes a shot at 6NT: the five-card club suit is probably worth a point and all his values are prime cards.

All will be well if the clubs behave — or if the king of hearts is a winner — but you know your luck. You win the first trick in hand, cash the ♣A-Q, and guess what happens . . .

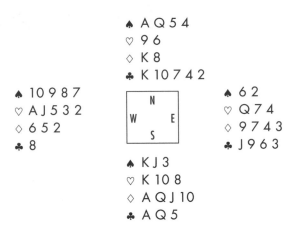

```
              ♠ A Q 5 4
              ♡ 9 6
              ◇ K 8
              ♣ K 10 7 4 2
♠ 10 9 8 7    ┌─────────┐    ♠ 6 2
♡ A J 5 3 2   │    N    │    ♡ Q 7 4
◇ 6 5 2       │ W     E │    ◇ 9 7 4 3
♣ 8           │    S    │    ♣ J 9 6 3
              └─────────┘
              ♠ K J 3
              ♡ K 10 8
              ◇ A Q J 10
              ♣ A Q 5
```

You are playing in 6NT and find the clubs 4-1 offside.
Now you just cash non-club winners, reaching this position:

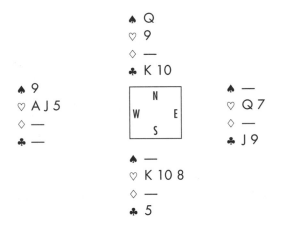

```
              ♠ Q
              ♡ 9
              ◇ —
              ♣ K 10
♠ 9           ┌─────────┐    ♠ —
♡ A J 5       │    N    │    ♡ Q 7
◇ —           │ W     E │    ◇ —
♣ —           │    S    │    ♣ J 9
              └─────────┘
              ♠ —
              ♡ K 10 8
              ◇ —
              ♣ 5
```

You lead the ♠Q from dummy, East discarding the ♡7 and South
the ♡8. You hope to find East with the ♡A, but when you lead
dummy's nine the queen appears, which is just as good. You
duck to endplay East and force him to reflect on the fact that he
should have thrown the ♡Q and kept the seven — singleton high
cards, under the strong hand, often become a liability.

Unfortunate Block

♠ 9 6 3
♡ K 10
◇ 7 5
♣ Q J 10 6 5 3

```
        N
  W         E
        S
```

♠ 10 led

♠ A Q
♡ Q 7 5 2
◇ K Q J 10 9
♣ A K

Dealer East
Neither vul.

WEST	NORTH	EAST	SOUTH
		1♠	dbl
pass	2♣	pass	2NT
pass	3NT	all pass	

You have too much for a 1NT overcall and, in any event, the hand seems nicely suited to play in a trump contract. For example, if North's assets consisted of ◇A-x-x-x-x and a singleton heart, you would want to reach 6◇.

West leads a spade to the seven and queen. Eight tricks look easy enough, but where can the ninth come from?

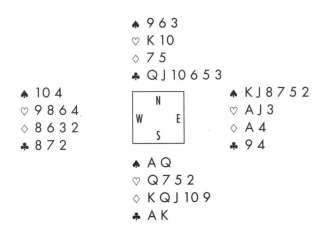

```
              ♠ 9 6 3
              ♡ K 10
              ◇ 7 5
              ♣ Q J 10 6 5 3
♠ 10 4          ┌─────────┐        ♠ K J 8 7 5 2
♡ 9 8 6 4       │    N    │        ♡ A J 3
◇ 8 6 3 2       │ W     E │        ◇ A 4
♣ 8 7 2         │    S    │        ♣ 9 4
                └─────────┘
              ♠ A Q
              ♡ Q 7 5 2
              ◇ K Q J 10 9
              ♣ A K
```

You play in 3NT after East has opened the bidding 1♠. West leads the ten of spades, which runs to the queen.

Although you had a likely eight tricks in your own hand, you called only 2NT over North's 2♣ because (a) he was forced to bid and might have nothing, and (b) you anticipated a blockage in clubs. You were right about the second point!

You can knock out the ace of diamonds now, but then the defenders will clear the spades and you will have nowhere to go for a ninth trick. You may think of playing the ♣A-K, followed by a heart to the ten. That sounds splendid, except that East holds the ♡J.

It is curiously difficult to see the advantage of playing off the ♣A-K and following with the *queen* of hearts. What can East do? If he wins, dummy gains an entry to the long clubs, giving you six clubs, two spades and the king of hearts; if he ducks, you switch to diamonds, again with nine tricks on top once the ace has gone.

If East turns up with 6-5 in the majors, he can presumably defeat you with four heart tricks and a diamond, but this sounds rather unlikely.

Amazing, Holmes!

```
        ♠ 9 6 5 2
        ♡ 8 6 3
        ◇ J 7
        ♣ A 8 6 2

              ┌─────────┐
              │    N    │
 ♡4 led       │ W     E │
              │    S    │
              └─────────┘

        ♠ A Q J 10 7 4
        ♡ A 10
        ◇ Q 10 9
        ♣ Q 4
```

Dealer East
N–S vul.

WEST	NORTH	EAST	SOUTH
		pass	1♠
pass	2♠	pass	3♠
all pass			

Your 3♠ was a game try, and it suggested that your hand was
fairly balanced. This bid comes in useful sometimes, telling partner he may place a value on all high cards. Although we know
that some players treat 3♠ in this sequence as a defensive move,
this agreement seems of marginal worth in these days of weak
two-bids.

Anyway, it's nice to have a partscore deal for once. West
leads the ♡4 and East plays the king. How should you plan the
play? See if you can assemble all the likely inferences.

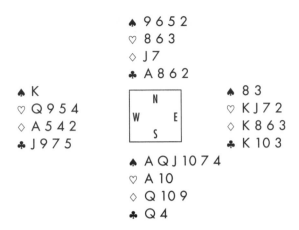

                      ♠ 9 6 5 2
                      ♡ 8 6 3
                      ◇ J 7
                      ♣ A 8 6 2
    ♠ K   ♠ 8 3
    ♡ Q 9 5 4   N   ♡ K J 7 2
    ◇ A 5 4 2   W   E   ◇ K 8 6 3
    ♣ J 9 7 5   S   ♣ K 10 3
                      ♠ A Q J 10 7 4
                      ♡ A 10
                      ◇ Q 10 9
                      ♣ Q 4

Your game try of 3♠ was borderline and, after a heart lead to the king and ace, you see five possible losers. The contract looks likely to depend upon how the trumps behave.

The play to the first trick suggests that East holds the king and jack of hearts, because West would not have led low from ♡Q-J. (The jack is often a better card for East to play in this type of situation, but that's another matter.)

East figures to hold one of the top diamonds, since with ◇A-K West would have had a better lead than from ♡Q-x-x-x. When you add this information to the fact that East passed as dealer (did you remember that?) it may occur to you that if he has the king of clubs, he can hardly hold the king of spades.

So, having won the initial heart, you make the surprise lead of the queen of clubs! Finding East with the king, you play West for the singleton king of trumps. There is no need to explain why — though you may feel sorely tempted!

Finally, if partner says it would have been easier to play a level lower, you can point out that West, with his 1-4-4-4 shape, would probably have doubled 2♠ for takeout.

Embarrassing Moment

> ♠ K 5
> ♡ 8 7 3
> ◇ K J 8 7 5 2
> ♣ A 3

♡ 10 led

	N	
W		E
	S	

> ♠ Q 10 7 6 2
> ♡ A Q
> ◇ A 9 3
> ♣ J 7 5

Dealer North
N–S vul.

WEST	NORTH	EAST	SOUTH
	1◇	1♡	1♠
pass	2◇	pass	3NT
all pass			

The current trend amongst duplicate players is to play that your free bid of 1♠ promises a five-card suit. With only four, you would make a negative double, which strongly suggests four spades, but it can include a hand with no other suitable bid — a flat shape with no heart stopper, maybe.

West's lead of the ten of hearts runs to your queen. It should not prove too difficult to find nine tricks, but bear in mind that East has overcalled in hearts and that you probably cannot afford to lose the lead more than once.

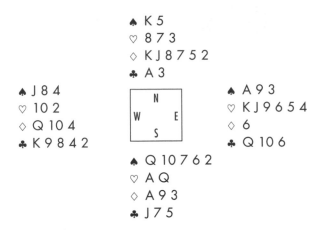

```
                      ♠ K 5
                      ♡ 8 7 3
                      ◇ K J 8 7 5 2
                      ♣ A 3
    ♠ J 8 4                              ♠ A 9 3
    ♡ 10 2              N                ♡ K J 9 6 5 4
    ◇ Q 10 4      W          E           ◇ 6
    ♣ K 9 8 4 2              S           ♣ Q 10 6
                      ♠ Q 10 7 6 2
                      ♡ A Q
                      ◇ A 9 3
                      ♣ J 7 5
```

You play in 3NT after North has bid and rebid diamonds. East overcalled in hearts and you have shown five spades. West leads the ten of hearts to the six and queen.

As the cards lie, you could make the contract simply by cashing the ace of diamonds and finessing the jack. Of course, this would not look so clever if East had ◇Q-x. If you lose a diamond early, you will have only eight tricks after East knocks out your second heart stopper. You will go down unless the hearts split 6-2 and West holds the spade ace. For the same reason you can forget about possible safety plays in diamonds.

Instead, cross to the king of diamonds and lead a small spade from the table. This will prove uncomfortable for East if he holds any of ♠A-J, ♠A-x-x or ♠A-9-x-x. If he goes up with the ace, you will have nine tricks without needing to bring in the long diamonds, and if he plays low, you will go up with the queen and play on diamonds with a carefree air.

On an initial club lead, you would have needed to guess the diamond position, but who could blame West for leading his partner's suit?

Club Cocktail

```
          ♠ K Q 6 5
          ♡ A 8 5 2
          ◇ Q
          ♣ J 9 6 5
```

```
              N
  ♠3 led    W   E
              S
```

```
          ♠ A J 10 9 7 2
          ♡ 10 4
          ◇ A 5
          ♣ Q 4 3
```

Dealer South
Both vul.

WEST	NORTH	EAST	SOUTH
			1♠
pass	4◇	pass	4♠
all pass			

North's 4◇ signified the values for a raise to 4♠ with a singleton or void in diamonds and at least four trumps. This is known as a 'splinter' and almost all experts play it. So often the ability to make a slam depends on how well the hands fit, and this method allows the opener to value a holding like A-x-x-x highly and to downgrade K-Q-x. As it happens, South has a minimum and signs off.

Knowing that dummy's attributes include a ruffing value, West leads a trump and East follows suit. It would be awful to lose a heart and three clubs, wouldn't it?

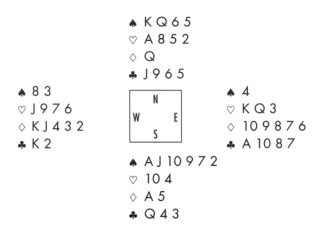

Playing in 4♠ on a trump lead, your first idea may be to draw trumps, strip the red suits and play a club to the queen.

There is a better line: after drawing the second trump, lead a small heart from dummy; when they return a red suit, ruff out the hearts and diamonds to reach here with South on lead:

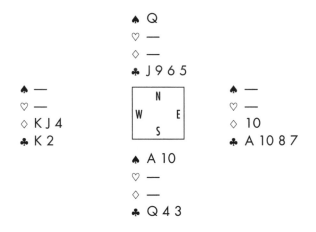

Now lead a club to the nine, succeeding whenever West has the ten and also when East holds A-10-x-x, K-10-x-x, A-10 or K-10 (because somebody will have to give you a ruff and discard).

Calamity Avoided

♠ A
♡ A K 8 6 4 2
◇ Q J 9 5
♣ 10 6

♠4 led

♠ J 7
♡ J 5
◇ K 10 8 6 2
♣ A K Q 3

Dealer South
Both vul.

WEST	NORTH	EAST	SOUTH
			1◇
pass	2♡	pass	3♣
pass	3◇	pass	4♣
pass	4♠	pass	5♣
pass	6◇	all pass	

This was good bidding to a good contract, but you have to take care of one or two possible losers besides the ace of trumps. With friendly breaks around, you should be able to set up the hearts, but you would like to find some other chances.

You win the first spade and advance the jack of diamonds, on which both opponents follow small. How do you continue? Don't stop your answer half way.

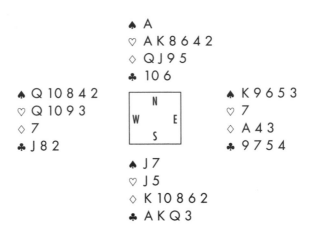

♠ A
♡ A K 8 6 4 2
◇ Q J 9 5
♣ 10 6

♠ Q 10 8 4 2
♡ Q 10 9 3
◇ 7
♣ J 8 2

N
W　E
S

♠ K 9 6 5 3
♡ 7
◇ A 4 3
♣ 9 7 5 4

♠ J 7
♡ J 5
◇ K 10 8 6 2
♣ A K Q 3

You are in 6◇ and the ♠A and ◇J win the first two tricks.

It could prove costly to lead a second trump, because an opponent who still held A-x might play two rounds. So before touching trumps again lead a club to the king, ruff a spade, return with a club and ruff your low club. The position is now:

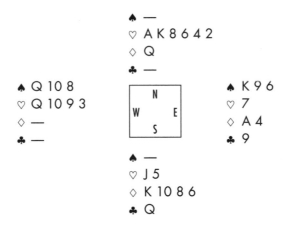

♠ —
♡ A K 8 6 4 2
◇ Q
♣ —

♠ Q 10 8
♡ Q 10 9 3
◇ —
♣ —

N
W　E
S

♠ K 9 6
♡ 7
◇ A 4
♣ 9

♠ —
♡ J 5
◇ K 10 8 6
♣ Q

You are in dummy and want to play a second round of trumps — *but cash the ace of hearts first.* Wouldn't it be awful if East captured the diamond and returned his singleton heart? You would be locked in dummy, forced to lead a heart for him to ruff!

Correct Assumption

          ♠ A K 9 3 2
          ♡ 7 4
          ♢ 10 9 4
          ♣ K 7 6

♡J led

	N	
W		E
	S	

          ♠ —
          ♡ A K 2
          ♢ A K J 8 6 2
          ♣ 9 8 5 4

Dealer East
Both vul.

WEST	NORTH	EAST	SOUTH
		pass	1♢
pass	1♠	pass	2♣
pass	3♢	pass	3NT
all pass			

We understand if you dislike South's rebid of 2♣ with such disparity of strength in the minor suits, but a successful international pair conducted this auction and we do not wish to argue. We surmise that South didn't fancy 3♢ with a void in spades and knew 2♢ was an underbid.

West leads the jack of hearts and East encourages with the nine. There seem to be plenty of tricks and no great danger, but your spade void may make entries difficult. Should you win the first trick, and how should you play when you gain the lead?

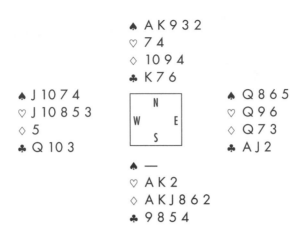

$\spadesuit$ A K 9 3 2
$\heartsuit$ 7 4
$\diamond$ 10 9 4
$\clubsuit$ K 7 6

$\spadesuit$ J 10 7 4
$\heartsuit$ J 10 8 5 3
$\diamond$ 5
$\clubsuit$ Q 10 3

$\spadesuit$ Q 8 6 5
$\heartsuit$ Q 9 6
$\diamond$ Q 7 3
$\clubsuit$ A J 2

$\spadesuit$ —
$\heartsuit$ A K 2
$\diamond$ A K J 8 6 2
$\clubsuit$ 9 8 5 4

You play in 3NT and West leads the jack of hearts.

It looks dangerous to hold off the first trick, because then you might find yourself losing a heart, a diamond and three clubs. Therefore, you take the $\heartsuit$K. Then a small problem arises at the next trick. Suppose you lay down the $\diamond$A and follow with a small one. East wins and plays another heart. Whether you win this or not you will go down if the opponents defend correctly.

To play off the ace and king of diamonds early on also fails. As before, East will lead a heart when he comes in.

The safe play, as you will have gauged by now, is to lead a *small* diamond. If the opponents win and play a heart, you can cross to the diamond ten and cash two spades.

There is a small story attached to this deal, which comes from the final of the 1992 Olympiad at Salsomaggiore. Writing for the *Daily Bulletin*, Terence Reese had to describe the play in the closed room before he had been able to discover what had actually happened. Taking a chance, he said that Hervé Mouiel had led a small diamond after winning the heart. He was right!

At the other table, the Americans reached the inferior contract of 5$\diamond$ and went one down; so, we will never know whether they would have found the winning line.

Clear the Air

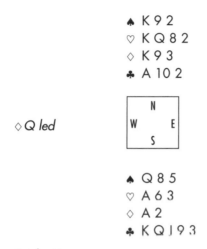

♠ K 9 2
♡ K Q 8 2
◇ K 9 3
♣ A 10 2

◇ Q led

```
      N
   W     E
      S
```

♠ Q 8 5
♡ A 6 3
◇ A 2
♣ K Q J 9 3

Dealer East
Neither vul.

WEST	NORTH	EAST	SOUTH
		3♠	3NT
pass	4♠	pass	5♣
pass	6NT	all pass	

By bidding 4♠ on the way to 6NT, North attempted to convey possibilities of a grand slam should you be in the upper range for your 3NT overcall.

West leads the queen of diamonds. There are ten tricks on top, an eleventh readily available in spades, and a number of possibilities for the twelfth. Your partner is going to feel very disappointed if you fail to make this contract.

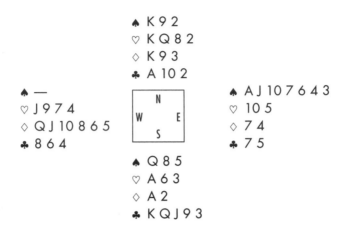

```
              ♠ K 9 2
              ♡ K Q 8 2
              ◇ K 9 3
              ♣ A 10 2
♠ —                            ♠ A J 10 7 6 4 3
♡ J 9 7 4        N             ♡ 10 5
◇ Q J 10 8 6 5  W    E         ◇ 7 4
♣ 8 6 4          S             ♣ 7 5
              ♠ Q 8 5
              ♡ A 6 3
              ◇ A 2
              ♣ K Q J 9 3
```

You play in 6NT after East has opened 3♠.

West leads the queen of diamonds and you win in hand with the ace. There are ten immediate winners and an eleventh to be had in spades. It may seem natural to cross to dummy and lead a small spade to the queen. After that, you may be able to find a way to embarrass West, or perhaps the heart suit will break kindly.

However, this sequence defies the general principle that most squeezes operate more easily when you are in a position to win all remaining tricks but one. It is better technique, therefore, to begin with a small spade to the king and ace. Whatever East does now, it will prove a simple matter to squeeze West in diamonds and hearts.

True, these days East might have held length in hearts. In that case, it would be easy to squeeze him in the majors. For the last four tricks, you will keep one spade and three hearts in hand, with four hearts still in dummy.

Finally, if you think East might have ◇ 10-x-x, you could play for a double squeeze instead. For this you would need to cash hearts rather than diamonds. You can't have it all!

Second Best

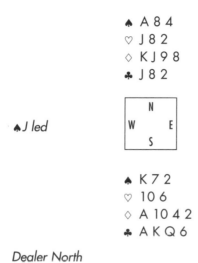

♠ A 8 4
♡ J 8 2
◇ K J 9 8
♣ J 8 2

♠ J led

♠ K 7 2
♡ 10 6
◇ A 10 4 2
♣ A K Q 6

Dealer North
N–S vul.

WEST	NORTH	EAST	SOUTH
	pass	pass	1NT¹
pass	3NT	all pass	

1. 15-17

West leads a spade and you foresee the happy prospect of ten
tricks so long as you can find the queen of diamonds.

You could begin by playing four rounds of clubs to see if anything interesting turns up. If you find a defender short in clubs,
he may be more likely to hold the ◇Q; also, if you sense that
someone has difficulty in discarding, you may feel inclined to
place him with this vital card. What is your best strategy?

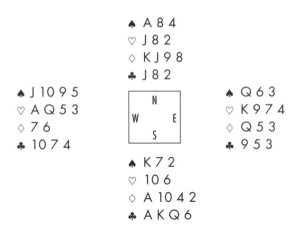

♠ A 8 4
♡ J 8 2
◇ K J 9 8
♣ J 8 2

♠ J 10 9 5
♡ A Q 5 3
◇ 7 6
♣ 10 7 4

♠ Q 6 3
♡ K 9 7 4
◇ Q 5 3
♣ 9 5 3

♠ K 7 2
♡ 10 6
◇ A 10 4 2
♣ A K Q 6

After a simple sequence, you reach 3NT. West leads the ♠J.

Two small clues point in opposite directions. Since West probably has ♠J-10-9 and East the queen, this leaves East more room to hold the queen of diamonds. As against that, East might possibly hold ♡A-K-Q, in which case his pass in second seat marks West with the ◇Q.

Someone good at finesses would take ten rapid tricks, but you are not so lucky. One idea is to win the spade in dummy and run the nine of diamonds. Then, if West wins with the queen, he may not find the heart switch. We rate another line more highly, however: win the spade in hand and run the ten of diamonds. East wins, but isn't it fairly certain that he will return his partner's suit, all the more so as he will expect West to hold the ace of diamonds? He may also reason that if you were afraid of a heart shift then you would have taken the finesse into his partner's hand.

When the match is over, an opponent who has found the queen of diamonds and made an overtrick may be pleased to say that he has made one more trick than the so-called expert.

On this deal, a heart lead would have been trickier, forcing you to guess the diamonds. However, it rarely pays to lead from A-Q-x-x when the declarer has shown a strong balanced hand.

Worry for West

♠ Q 9 6 2
♡ 10 4
◇ A 9 3
♣ 9 5 3 2

♠ J led

```
      N
  W       E
      S
```

♠ —
♡ K 7
◇ K 7 6 5 4 2
♣ A K Q 8 6

Dealer East
Both vul.

WEST	NORTH	EAST	SOUTH
		pass	1◇
pass	1♠	pass	2♣
pass	2◇	pass	3♣
pass	4♣	pass	5◇
all pass			

It is not easy to bid these hands with any confidence. You must hope that partner has some values in a red suit. You might have preferred 5♣ but perhaps feared running into a ruff if the ace of diamonds was missing.

West leads the jack of spades and you ruff. Since the heart situation looks unpromising, you may think at first that you will need to find the diamonds 2-2. Is there another chance?

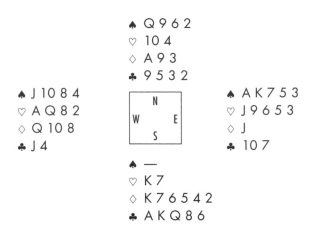

```
              ♠ Q 9 6 2
              ♡ 10 4
              ◇ A 9 3
              ♣ 9 5 3 2
♠ J 10 8 4          N          ♠ A K 7 5 3
♡ A Q 8 2                      ♡ J 9 6 5 3
◇ Q 10 8    W          E       ◇ J
♣ J 4              S           ♣ 10 7
              ♠ —
              ♡ K 7
              ◇ K 7 6 5 4 2
              ♣ A K Q 8 6
```

You play in 5◇ after East has passed as dealer and the opponents have not entered the bidding. West leads the jack of spades, which you ruff. You play the king and ace of diamonds and East shows out.

You can do better than rely on the heart position, which will probably be wrong because (a) West must have had a good reason not to lead the unbid suit and (b) East, who passed originally, seems more or less marked with the top spades. In dummy, after taking the second trump, ruff a spade and play off your winning clubs. West does not make the mistake of ruffing, which would enable you to get rid of a heart from dummy on the fifth club and obtain a heart ruff.

Win the fourth club in dummy, ruff a spade and play the fifth club, ruffing with the ◇9. This brings you down to two hearts and one diamond, while West, with fear in his heart, is probably clutching the ◇Q and ♡A-Q. (You would normally manage to read it if he has bared his ace of hearts.) When you ruff dummy's last spade, West overruffs and you make a trick in hearts after all. Well played everyone!

Quick Decision

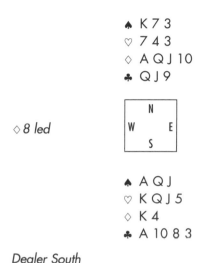

♠ K 7 3
♡ 7 4 3
◇ A Q J 10
♣ Q J 9

◇ 8 led

	N	
W		E
	S	

♠ A Q J
♡ K Q J 5
◇ K 4
♣ A 10 8 3

Dealer South
Neither vul.

WEST	NORTH	EAST	SOUTH
			2NT
pass	6NT	all pass	

From North's viewpoint, the contract might play a trick better in diamonds if South holds, for example, A-x in one the majors; however, unless you play a complicated relay system, it can prove very difficult to find out about these things. Even if you had the tools available, the information given away on normal hands tends to offset the occasional gain.

There will be no problem if the club finesse succeeds and, apparently, no hope if it loses. Is there any stratagem that may enable you to succeed when West has the king of clubs?

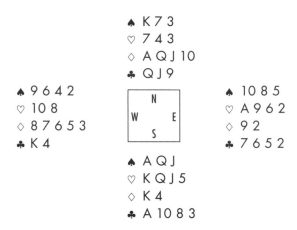

```
                    ♠ K 7 3
                    ♡ 7 4 3
                    ◇ A Q J 10
                    ♣ Q J 9
    ♠ 9 6 4 2         ┌─────────┐         ♠ 10 8 5
    ♡ 10 8            │    N    │         ♡ A 9 6 2
    ◇ 8 7 6 5 3       │ W     E │         ◇ 9 2
    ♣ K 4             │    S    │         ♣ 7 6 5 2
                      └─────────┘
                    ♠ A Q J
                    ♡ K Q J 5
                    ◇ K 4
                    ♣ A 10 8 3
```

You reach 6NT after an uninformative auction. West leads the
eight of diamonds. Would you shrug your shoulders and risk all
on the club finesse?

It seems you must, but a possibility exists that East may duck
two rounds of hearts. You win the first trick with the ten of diamonds and lead a heart to the queen, which holds as West plays
the eight. You quickly go back to dummy with a diamond and
lead another heart.

It is surely possible that East will play low again, because
from his angle you might have a guess at this point. If the king
of hearts wins this trick, you cross to the king of spades and take
the club finesse, for a possible overtrick!

If West complains (as players do), East may reply: 'I had to
make a quick decision. I placed declarer with something like:

♠ A J x (or A Q x)   ♡ K Q 10 x   ◇ K x x   ♣ A K x

You wouldn't have felt very happy if I had gone up with the ace
of hearts and crashed your jack.'

Hidden Danger

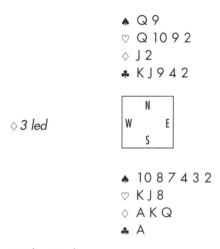

♠ Q 9
♡ Q 10 9 2
◇ J 2
♣ K J 9 4 2

◇ *3 led*

	N	
W		E
	S	

♠ 10 8 7 4 3 2
♡ K J 8
◇ A K Q
♣ A

Dealer South
Neither vul.

WEST	NORTH	EAST	SOUTH
			1♠
pass	1NT	pass	3♠
pass	4♠	all pass	

The rebid of 3♠ is a trifle awkward on the South hand because
players who respond 1NT to 1♠ often hold a singleton spade.
Still, no sensible alternative presents itself. There are greater
flaws attached to both 2◇ and 2NT.

West leads a small diamond to the nine and ace. The initial
problem is how to play the spades, assuming that West plays low
second in hand. There is another, more subtle, point in the play,
one you must take care not to overlook.

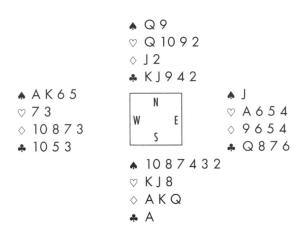

```
                    ♠ Q 9
                    ♡ Q 10 9 2
                    ◇ J 2
                    ♣ K J 9 4 2
♠ A K 6 5          ┌──────────┐        ♠ J
♡ 7 3              │    N     │        ♡ A 6 5 4
◇ 10 8 7 3         │ W     E  │        ◇ 9 6 5 4
♣ 10 5 3           │    S     │        ♣ Q 8 7 6
                   └──────────┘
                    ♠ 10 8 7 4 3 2
                    ♡ K J 8
                    ◇ A K Q
                    ♣ A
```

You play in 4♠ and West leads a diamond to the nine and ace.

There are at least three immediate losers and you have to consider how to play from dummy when West plays low on the first round of trumps. Should you play the queen or the nine? The nine gains when West holds J-6 or J-5; the queen gains when East holds J-6 or J-5; the added chance that East may hold the singleton jack makes it right to put up dummy's queen.

So, is that all? No, if you play a spade to the queen and return a spade, West may switch to his doubleton heart. East will hold off the first round and later give his partner a ruff. Now you will regret that you didn't think of cashing the ace of clubs before leading a trump; this would have enabled you to discard a heart on the king of clubs and so escape the ruff. Of course, East could still play a third round of hearts, but your trumps are just good enough to allow you to ruff high.

An opening heart lead would have beaten the contract and perhaps in view of your jump rebid West might have worked out that a forcing game stood little chance of success. All the same, a heart lead could easily have damaged East's holding and you cannot seriously fault his choice.

Lie Down Dead

```
              ♠ J 10 6 2
              ♡ 6 4 3
              ◇ J 6 2
              ♣ A J 5

                    ┌─────────┐
                    │    N    │
  ◇ 7 led           │ W     E │
                    │    S    │
                    └─────────┘

              ♠ A K Q 7 4 3
              ♡ K 7 5 2
              ◇ —
              ♣ K 10 4
```

Dealer South
E–W vul.

WEST	NORTH	EAST	SOUTH
			1♠
pass	2♠	pass	4♠
all pass			

This time you have no doubt about your spades and you happily jump to game after the single raise. One can just about construct a hand for North that will make a slam good (A-Q-x-x opposite one of the kings and Q-x opposite the other), but it rarely pays to go in search of the perfect fit.

You ruff the initial diamond and lead a trump to the jack, to which all follow. It would be unlucky now to lose three heart tricks and a trick to the queen of clubs as well. In fact, partner would think it worse than that — almost unforgivable.

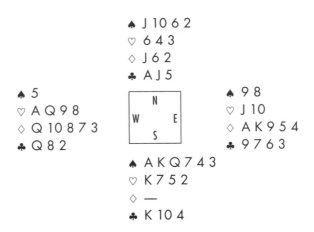

Playing in 4♠, you ruff the diamond and play a trump.

Using the ♠J-10 as entries, you should eliminate diamonds and then exit with a heart; this leaves East on play in this position:

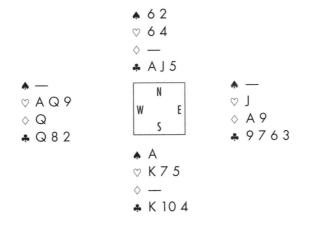

East leads the ♡J and you lie down dead, playing the five. No matter how the hearts lie, this ensures the contract. If they break 3-3, the long heart will provide a club discard. If East has four hearts, he will have to yield a trick to the king, break open the clubs or yield a ruff-and-discard.

Last Chance

♠ Q
♡ A K J 8 3 2
◇ 9 7 6 5 2
♣ 6

♠ J led

```
      N
   W     E
      S
```

♠ A K 6 4
♡ 6 5
◇ A K
♣ A Q 10 8 2

Dealer South
Neither vul.

WEST	NORTH	EAST	SOUTH
			1♣
pass	1♡	pass	2♠
pass	3♡	pass	3NT
pass	4◇	pass	4♡
pass	5♡	pass	6NT
all pass			

Your partner has a train to catch and you will not be able to finish the rubber. This could be your last chance to shine, and you are delighted to find yourself playing a slam.

The spade lead removes a side entry for the hearts, which is a pity. Unless you strike it lucky and make six tricks in hearts, you will have to find an extra trick from somewhere.

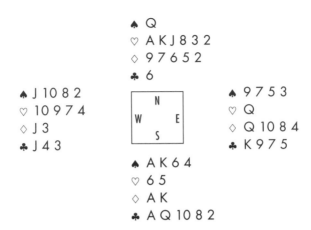

After a lengthy auction, you reach 6NT. West leads the jack of spades, which seems a little unfortunate for your side because of the awkward entry situation.

It would not seem too unreasonable to cross to the ace of diamonds and finesse the jack of hearts. If this loses to the queen, you will need the hearts to break and also a winning club finesse in order to arrive at twelve tricks. Still, as this is a slam contract, you must make a special effort.

If you can make six tricks in hearts, you will not need the club finesse, but still it can't cost to establish the club position before you tackle the hearts. The first play, therefore, should be a club to the queen, which holds.

Now you require only five heart tricks and it may seem natural to finesse the jack. Now wait a minute — this cannot help you to make the contract — if the hearts are going to break 3-2, you won't need six tricks from the suit. Have you got there now? It cannot cost to duck the first round, thereby giving yourself the extra chance of bringing down a singleton queen.

Hasty Action

```
               ♠ A 6 3
               ♡ A Q 9
               ♢ Q J 8 7 3
               ♣ 7 6

                  ┌─────────┐
                  │    N    │
    ♣2 led        │ W     E │
                  │    S    │
                  └─────────┘

               ♠ K J 5 4
               ♡ K J 3
               ♢ 10 9
               ♣ A J 9 4
```

Dealer North
Both vul.

WEST	NORTH	EAST	SOUTH
	1♢	pass	1♠
pass	2♠	pass	3NT
all pass			

The auction seems well judged. Holding three-card spade support, a ruffing value and no club stopper, North's raise to 2♠ was much better than 1NT. Taking account of the fact that North might have only three trumps, you rebid 3NT to offer a choice of contracts.

West leads the two of clubs (playing third and fifth leads) and East puts up the ten. How should you plan the play?

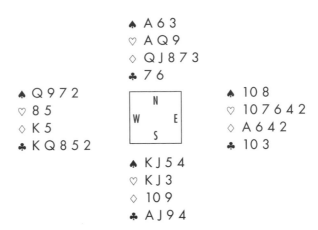

```
              ♠ A 6 3
              ♡ A Q 9
              ◇ Q J 8 7 3
              ♣ 7 6
♠ Q 9 7 2                          ♠ 10 8
♡ 8 5          N                   ♡ 10 7 6 4 2
◇ K 5      W       E               ◇ A 6 4 2
♣ K Q 8 5 2        S               ♣ 10 3
              ♠ K J 5 4
              ♡ K J 3
              ◇ 10 9
              ♣ A J 9 4
```

You play in 3NT and West leads the two of clubs (surely fifth highest from a five-card suit) to East's ten.

It looks obvious to capture the ♣10 with the jack, but let us see what happens. Keen to preserve his partner's entry, East wins the first diamond and returns a club, allowing West to finesse the eight. You have one further club stopper with the ace, but the ◇K gives a sure entry to the long clubs.

Now watch the effect of ducking the first trick. East returns a club and your jack loses to the queen. West can switch now, restricting you to one club trick, but this one suffices.

It is no better for the defenders if East follows the ♣10 with the ♠10. You can let this run to dummy's ace, knock out the ◇K, and go up with the king on the second spade. No matter how the spades lie, you will only lose at most one spade trick.

Yes, holding up loses if both diamond entries turn up on your left. However, other things being equal, East figures to hold at least one top diamond — particularly since West might have overcalled with five decent clubs and the ◇A-K; players do that.

Knowing West's club length helped you here, but this is not why we dislike third and fifth leads. Their real drawback is that East cannot tell whether West has strength in the suit.

Simple Precaution

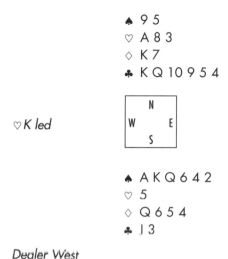

```
              ♠ 9 5
              ♡ A 8 3
              ◇ K 7
              ♣ K Q 10 9 5 4

                   ┌─────────┐
                   │    N    │
    ♡ K led        │ W     E │
                   │    S    │
                   └─────────┘

              ♠ A K Q 6 4 2
              ♡ 5
              ◇ Q 6 5 4
              ♣ J 3
```

Dealer West
Neither vul.

WEST	NORTH	EAST	SOUTH
2♡	3♣	3♡	4♠
all pass			

West's weak two opening promised a six-card heart suit and something like 6-9 points. You might have bid only 3♠ but it is hard to see how you would play other than in the spade game; the less you reveal about your hand, the greater the chance of a defensive error.

You win the opening lead in dummy and have two main options: aim for a diamond ruff or hope to bring in the clubs. What is your line?

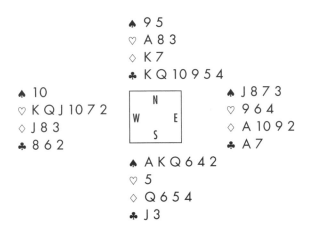

```
                    ♠ 9 5
                    ♡ A 8 3
                    ◇ K 7
                    ♣ K Q 10 9 5 4
  ♠ 10                               ♠ J 8 7 3
  ♡ K Q J 10 7 2        N            ♡ 9 6 4
  ◇ J 8 3           W       E        ◇ A 10 9 2
  ♣ 8 6 2               S            ♣ A 7
                    ♠ A K Q 6 4 2
                    ♡ 5
                    ◇ Q 6 5 4
                    ♣ J 3
```

Against 4♠, West leads the ♡K, won in dummy.

If trumps break 3-2, one diamond ruff will suffice, but a 4-1 break will put you in trouble if you attack diamonds.

Suppose you rely on the clubs and draw three rounds of trumps. West will show out on the second, leaving East with a master trump. If you now play a club to the king, East will see West's count signal and hold up for one round. He will take the next club and exit with a major-suit card to leave you two down.

You might think of giving East his trump trick after the A-K-Q. If he returns a heart, you have him. You ruff, and then, after winning the first club in dummy, you ruff another heart and continue clubs. East will have no happy return when he wins the second round. Of course, he can avoid this by returning either a small club or a diamond when he is in with his trump trick. You are nearly there . . .

You need to observe the simple precaution of taking the first heart ruff straight away; you will ruff a second after dummy wins the first club. This way, when East gets in with the ace of clubs, he is dead. Cashing his trump is no good and if he returns a diamond, he must play another after ruffing a club; either way you lose only a diamond, a trump and a club.

Memories of '66

```
          ♠ A K
          ♡ J 9 2
          ◇ Q 7 3
          ♣ 10 8 6 5 2

              ┌─────────┐
              │    N    │
  ♠ 5 led     │ W     E │
              │    S    │
              └─────────┘

          ♠ 10 2
          ♡ A K 7 5
          ◇ A K 10
          ♣ J 9 7 3
```

Dealer South
Both vul.

WEST	NORTH	EAST	SOUTH
			1NT
pass	3NT	all pass	

Many Englishmen (Terence Reese included!) have fond memories of 1966, as it was the one time the England soccer team won the World Cup. It was also a year Jeremy Flint would remember well. In a whistle-stop tour of the USA, he won thirteen regional titles and became a Life Master in eleven weeks — a record that stood almost until his death.

Here, Flint, having opened a strong notrump with a losing doubleton, was faced with a seemingly impossible contract. However, he spotted a winning line and took it. Can you?

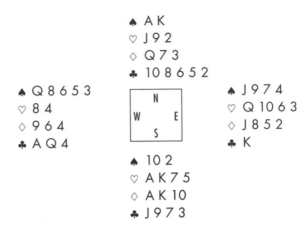

```
              ♠ A K
              ♡ J 9 2
              ◊ Q 7 3
              ♣ 10 8 6 5 2
♠ Q 8 6 5 3        N        ♠ J 9 7 4
♡ 8 4                       ♡ Q 10 6 3
◊ 9 6 4        W     E      ◊ J 8 5 2
♣ A Q 4            S        ♣ K
              ♠ 10 2
              ♡ A K 7 5
              ◊ A K 10
              ♣ J 9 7 3
```

You play in 3NT and West leads the five of spades.

Jeremy Flint could see that it would take almost a miracle for playing on clubs to give him nine tricks in time. As well as something like a 7-2 spade division or blockage, he would need a friendly club split. For example, the defender with the seven-card spade suit would need a club holding of a void, a singleton, or a doubleton queen. In any case, if the five of spades was an honest card, the only way spades could be 7-2 was if West had led from a doubleton.

Flint knew his opponents were good players, most unlikely to block the spades, and decided that trying to run four fast heart tricks represented a far better bet. Although he could have catered for a singleton queen with East, he reckoned that he stood a better chance playing West to be short in the suit. He was right.

He led the jack to pick up East's queen and returned to dummy with a diamond. He then led the nine, pinning West's eight and collecting the ten on the way. Finally, he went back over with a spade and confidently finessed the ♡5.

Safe Passage

```
          ♠ A 7 6
          ♡ 9 7 6 3
          ◇ A K Q 4
          ♣ Q 3

                ┌─────────┐
                │    N    │
♡ Q led         │ W     E │
                │    S    │
                └─────────┘

          ♠ Q 9 5
          ♡ A K
          ◇ 9 7
          ♣ K 9 7 6 5 4
```

Dealer South
N–S vul.

WEST	NORTH	EAST	SOUTH
			1♣
pass	1◇	pass	1NT
pass	3NT	all pass	

Quite rightly, North viewed his hearts as a suit only worth showing if you happened to bid them. You could have rebid 2♣ but,
with so much strength in the majors, 1NT (a weak rebid in your
system) seemed more descriptive.

On the lead of the ♡Q East follows with the two and your ace
wins. Hoping to catch West with the doubleton ace of clubs, you
start by leading a club to the queen. Alas, East wins with the ace
and returns the eight of hearts to your king. What should you do
next?

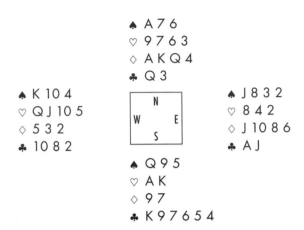

```
              ♠ A 7 6
              ♡ 9 7 6 3
              ◇ A K Q 4
              ♣ Q 3
♠ K 10 4          N          ♠ J 8 3 2
♡ Q J 10 5                   ♡ 8 4 2
◇ 5 3 2      W        E      ◇ J 10 8 6
♣ 10 8 2          S          ♣ A J
              ♠ Q 9 5
              ♡ A K
              ◇ 9 7
              ♣ K 9 7 6 5 4
```

Playing in 3NT, you receive a heart lead. You try a club to the queen, but East wins with the ace and returns a heart.

You could ask about the East-West carding methods. If you do, you are told the two on the first heart was not encouraging. So East may or may not have a third heart.

If East has two of the three missing clubs, the king of spades and no more hearts, you could make the contract (indeed an overtrick) by cashing the king of clubs and giving up the third round. The ♠Q will give you a late entry to the clubs. Can you see an improvement on this?

Well, West could hold length in clubs or the king of spades, and there is no special reason to expect the hearts to break 5-2. You can give yourself an extra chance by taking three rounds of diamonds before playing the king and another club. If the layout were as discussed above (where clearing the clubs straight away would have succeeded), East would score a club and a diamond or two but then be forced to lead from the ♠K. In practice, West wins the third round of clubs. Thankfully, hearts break 4-3, East has the last diamond and West the ♠K. Therefore, you lose just two hearts and a second club before the endplay works.

Sober Reflection

```
        ♠ 8 6
        ♡ A 8 7 6 5 2
        ◇ J 8 2
        ♣ K 6
```

```
              N
◇ 3 led      W    E
              S
```

```
        ♠ A K Q J 3 2
        ♡ Q
        ◇ K 9
        ♣ Q J 7 5
```

Dealer East
N–S vul.

WEST	NORTH	EAST	SOUTH
		3◇	4♠
all pass			

You might overcall 3♠ on a far weaker hand than this and, as you hardly want to encourage partner to bid hearts, the simple jump to game is probably best.

East wins the opening lead with the ace and you follow low. Dropping the king would fool nobody on this deal since West would hardly lead the three from 9-3 doubleton. East returns the ◇6 and, predictably, West ruffs your king before exiting with the ♠10. How should you continue?

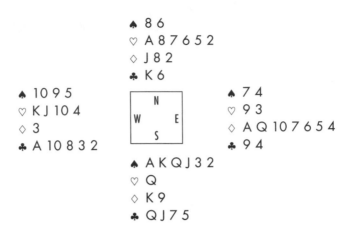

                    ♠ 8 6
                    ♡ A 8 7 6 5 2
                    ◇ J 8 2
                    ♣ K 6
    ♠ 10 9 5   ♠ 7 4
    ♡ K J 10 4   ♡ 9 3
    ◇ 3   ◇ A Q 10 7 6 5 4
    ♣ A 10 8 3 2   ♣ 9 4
                    ♠ A K Q J 3 2
                    ♡ Q
                    ◇ K 9
                    ♣ Q J 7 5

Playing in 4♠ after losing a diamond and a ruff, the original declarer attacked clubs. West won the second round and played another trump, scoring a further club at the end.

A moment's reflection will warn against trying to ruff a club. Surely, either West will draw dummy's trump or East will over-ruff. Instead run all but one of your trumps for a trump squeeze:

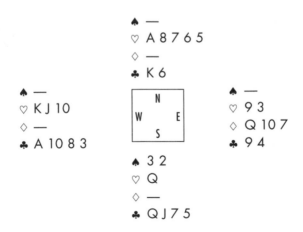

                    ♠ —
                    ♡ A 8 7 6 5
                    ◇ —
                    ♣ K 6
    ♠ —   ♠ —
    ♡ K J 10   ♡ 9 3
    ◇ —   ◇ Q 10 7
    ♣ A 10 8 3   ♣ 9 4
                    ♠ 3 2
                    ♡ Q
                    ◇ —
                    ♣ Q J 7 5

You can set up whichever suit West discards on your second-last trump.

Unusual Losers

♠ A 6 4
♡ Q J 10 9 5 3
♢ A Q 2
♣ A

♠ K led

```
    N
  W   E
    S
```

♠ 9 7 5
♡ K
♢ 5 3
♣ K Q J 10 9 8 2

Dealer West
E–W vul.

WEST	NORTH	EAST	SOUTH
3♠	4♡	pass	5♣
all pass			

At rubber bridge, you knew there was no danger that North might interpret 5♣ as a cuebid; it was simply a matter of deciding whether a club contract stood a realistic chance of playing two tricks better than a heart contract.

West leads the king of spades and it comes as no surprise when East trumps dummy's ace with the three of clubs. Without apparent thought, he returns the five of clubs.

It looks like you can knock out the ace of hearts, draw trumps and claim — or can you see a snag?

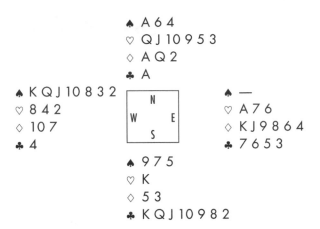

                   ♠ A 6 4
                   ♡ Q J 10 9 5 3
                   ◇ A Q 2
                   ♣ A

♠ K Q J 10 8 3 2   ♠ —
♡ 8 4 2   N   ♡ A 7 6
◇ 10 7   W   E   ◇ K J 9 8 6 4
♣ 4   S   ♣ 7 6 5 3

                   ♠ 9 7 5
                   ♡ K
                   ◇ 5 3
                   ♣ K Q J 10 9 8 2

You play in 5♣ after West opened 3♠. East ruffs dummy's ace of spades and returns a trump.

You must play a heart next and all will be well if East goes in with the ace, but what happens if he ducks? You might draw trumps and there is a chance that the diamond finesse will succeed. If it does, you can take a ruffing finesse against the ace of hearts and score an overtrick. Unfortunately, East holds the king of diamonds (hardly unexpected when West has so many spades) and you wind up two down.

Perhaps the fact that you might score an overtrick if you can manage to set up the hearts provides a clue. If it meant that you gained an entry to dummy, you could afford to lose a trick in one of the minors.

Aha! If East began with four trumps (or if he has carelessly played this way with 7-5-3), you can concede a trump to him and obtain the extra entry. Of course, this is only possible if you play something other than the two under the ace. Naturally, you are not going to play for an error (which ducking the first trump to cater for the 7-5-3 holding would be doing) when an excellent genuine chance exists. So, after the king of hearts wins, you draw a second round of trumps and concede the third.

Long Rubber

```
            ♠ A K 8
            ♡ 9 3
            ◊ 10 7 6 4 3
            ♣ J 5 4
```

```
            ┌─────────┐
            │    N    │
♡ 4 led     │ W     E │
            │    S    │
            └─────────┘
```

```
            ♠ 10 4 3
            ♡ K Q J 6
            ◊ Q 5 2
            ♣ A K Q
```

Dealer East
Both vul.

WEST	NORTH	EAST	SOUTH
		1 ◊	1NT
pass	2NT	pass	3NT
all pass			

It has been a long rubber, with both sides accumulating a series of small scores above the line, but now it seems the climax has arrived. You are in game and have a chance to wrap up the rubber.

East captures the nine of hearts with the ace and, with a resigned air, returns the seven. Can you see how to do it?

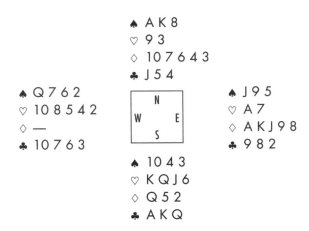

```
                    ♠ A K 8
                    ♡ 9 3
                    ◇ 10 7 6 4 3
                    ♣ J 5 4
    ♠ Q 7 6 2          N          ♠ J 9 5
    ♡ 10 8 5 4 2                  ♡ A 7
    ◇ —          W         E      ◇ A K J 9 8
    ♣ 10 7 6 3          S         ♣ 9 8 2
                    ♠ 10 4 3
                    ♡ K Q J 6
                    ◇ Q 5 2
                    ♣ A K Q
```

You play in 3NT and win the second round of hearts.

You suspect that West, to lead from a ragged heart suit, has a void in diamonds. East's apparent dismay at having his entry removed so early in the play seems to bear this out. However, the precise diamond layout is largely academic. The one thing you need to know, and which the opening bid more or less tells you, is that East holds the ace and king.

The original declarer, in a hurry to end the rubber swiftly, went down. He simply used the ace and king of spades as entries to lead diamonds twice and lost five tricks: two spades, one heart and two diamonds.

You have no other way to reach dummy than with the spades and no endplay presents itself, yet there is a path home. To shut out West's long spade you must duck a spade, either on the first round, or before going back to dummy. This play proves essential whenever East has J-x-x and also if he has Q-x-x and the foresight to unblock.

You wouldn't have missed the hold-up if West had led a spade, yet somehow the need to employ the same technique when you broach the suit is easier to overlook.

Full Value

```
        ♠ Q 5
        ♡ 10 4 3
        ◇ Q J 4 2
        ♣ K Q 10 6
```

```
            ┌─────────┐
            │    N    │
♠ 10 led    │ W     E │
            │    S    │
            └─────────┘
```

```
        ♠ A 6
        ♡ A Q J 6
        ◇ 10 6 5 3
        ♣ A J 5
```

Dealer South
Both vul.

WEST	NORTH	EAST	SOUTH
			1NT¹
pass	3NT	all pass	

1. 15-17

West leads the ♠10 and, annoyingly, dummy's queen loses to the
king. You hold up, not so much with any expectation of cutting
the defensive communications, but to learn more about the spade
layout. Interestingly, East returns the ♠J to your ace.

Even assuming the heart finesse works, you may still have
only eight tricks. Should you try to sneak through a diamond so
that three heart winners will do? What is the best line?

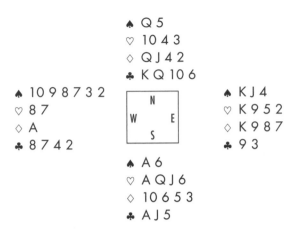

♠ Q 5
♥ 10 4 3
♦ Q J 4 2
♣ K Q 10 6

♠ 10 9 8 7 3 2
♥ 8 7
♦ A
♣ 8 7 4 2

♠ K J 4
♥ K 9 5 2
♦ K 9 8 7
♣ 9 3

♠ A 6
♥ A Q J 6
♦ 10 6 5 3
♣ A J 5

Playing in 3NT, you receive a spade lead. You try dummy's queen, but East plays the king, which you let hold. East then returns the jack.

Unless one defender holds the five missing spades and the other defender holds all the entries, attempting to set up the diamonds will result in defeat — they are not both about to duck a diamond. You need the heart finesse to work, but there is no need to rely on a 3-3 break. Normally you would aim to cater for ♥K-x onside. Here, a lack of entries makes it impossible.

You could start with a small heart off dummy and pick up a singleton king. However, there is a better line. After taking the ♠A and cashing the ♣A, cross to dummy cheaply with a club and lead the ♥10. East does best to cover and the ace wins. You note West's high card, cash one more heart, run the rest of the clubs and ultimately finesse the ♥6.

Leading the ten (and planning to finesse on the third round) gains on three West heart holdings: 9-8, 9-7 or 8-7; it only loses with two: 9-8-7 and 9-8-7-5-2. Moreover, given that the spades appear to be 6-3, the last of these seems rather unlikely. It was just as well that you were full value for your strong notrump with A-Q-J-6 of hearts and not A-Q-J-5!

familiar Ring

```
              ♠ Q 7 2
              ♡ 8 5 4
              ◇ A K 9
              ♣ K 6 5 4

              ┌─────────┐
              │    N    │
  ♠J led      │ W     E │
              │    S    │
              └─────────┘

              ♠ K
              ♡ A K 7 6 3
              ◇ 6 4 3 2
              ♣ A 9 2
```

Dealer East
Neither vul.

WEST	NORTH	EAST	SOUTH
		2♠	3♡
pass	4♡	all pass	

You would have doubled East's weak two if your five-card suit had been one of the minors. As it was, partner could have advanced with 3♠ over 3♡ to try for 3NT. This could avoid the danger of a ruff or an overruff and nine tricks might be the limit on the deal. This is all water under the bridge now and you must focus on making 4♡, which is surely the best spot.

East wins the first trick with the ace of spades and returns the six. How should you plan the play?

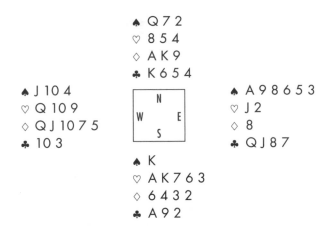

                    ♠ Q 7 2
                    ♡ 8 5 4
                    ◇ A K 9
                    ♣ K 6 5 4

♠ J 10 4   ♠ A 9 8 6 5 3
♡ Q 10 9   N   ♡ J 2
◇ Q J 10 7 5   W   E   ◇ 8
♣ 10 3   S   ♣ Q J 8 7

                    ♠ K
                    ♡ A K 7 6 3
                    ◇ 6 4 3 2
                    ♣ A 9 2

You play in 4♡ after East has shown a weak hand with a six-card spade suit. The defenders play two rounds of spades.

The deal has a familiar ring to it. If a long club will not take care of a loser, you could aim for a diamond ruff in dummy. The snag is that if you draw two rounds of trumps, whoever gets in with a diamond may play a third; if you pull only one round of trumps, the defenders may score a diamond ruff in the short trump hand. To get around this you might concede a diamond early, planning then to take two rounds of trumps. Unfortunately, the way the cards lie, East still gets a ruff.

Nobody will blame you for that line, but you might have made the contract nonetheless. You can ruff the spade return and cash the two top hearts followed by the ace and king of clubs. Then throw a club on the ♠Q, ruff a club, go back to dummy with a diamond and ruff another club. West can never gain by overruffing and this dummy reversal even lands the contract if he has a 3-4-2-4 shape. In this case you leave West fuming: he has to ruff his partner's winning diamond.

Single Minded

```
        ♠ Q 8 6 2
        ♡ K 9
        ◇ Q 10 8
        ♣ A 7 5 2

             ┌─────────┐
             │    N    │
♣ K led      │ W     E │
             │    S    │
             └─────────┘

        ♠ 7 4
        ♡ A Q J 10 8 7 2
        ◇ A
        ♣ 10 4 3
```

Dealer South
Both vul.

WEST	NORTH	EAST	SOUTH
			1♡
2NT	dbl	3◇	4♡
all pass			

West's unusual notrump, as we have said before, is a risky venture. If he runs into a misfit, your side might double and lead trumps. If not, you can often outbid him and use knowledge of his distribution to make the contract.

West leads the king of clubs and, knowing you would be in trouble if East ruffs dummy's ace of clubs, you inwardly heave a sigh of relief when he follows with the eight.

The bidding tells you not to play West for the ♣K-Q doubleton and the ♠A-K or East for the ♠A-K doubleton. Can you think of any layout that would enable you to succeed?

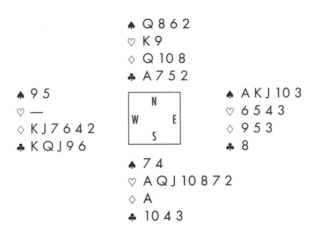

♠ Q 8 6 2
♡ K 9
◇ Q 10 8
♣ A 7 5 2

♠ 9 5
♡ —
◇ K J 7 6 4 2
♣ K Q J 9 6

♠ A K J 10 3
♡ 6 5 4 3
◇ 9 5 3
♣ 8

♠ 7 4
♡ A Q J 10 8 7 2
◇ A
♣ 10 4 3

Playing in 4♡ after West has announced the minors, you win the club lead in dummy.

If East has ◇K-J-x and gets it into his head that you have A-9 doubleton, he may play the jack if you lead the suit off dummy, allowing a later ruffing finesse. Do you wonder if there could be an endplay if East has ◇K-x-x and both top spades? With dummy's only side entry gone, you could only achieve a strip if trumps were 2-2. This is impossible as East would have opened with 11 points and a 7-2-3-1 shape.

Actually, an endplay is the answer, and you do need a 6-3 diamond break. You also need some luck in the spade suit. Unblock the diamond ace and use the king and nine of hearts as entries to ruff diamonds. Then run all your trumps, throwing clubs from dummy. Reduced to four cards, what can East do?

If he keeps ♠A-K-J-10, you can duck a spade to him and the queen is bound to score. If he keeps ♠A-K-J-x, you can afford to cover the nine if West plays it and again East has to concede a spade trick to dummy. The endplay would, of course, also work if East had ♠A-K-J-10-9. In that case you would not need the one-suit squeeze.

So Simple

```
        ♠ A Q J 10 7
        ♡ A 4
        ◇ Q 10 7 5 4 3
        ♣ —

              N
♣ 10 led   W     E
              S

        ♠ K 3
        ♡ K J 10 9 8 2
        ◇ A 6
        ♣ A J 8
```

Dealer North
N–S vul.

WEST	NORTH	EAST	SOUTH
	1♠	pass	3♡
pass	3♠	pass	3NT
pass	4♡	pass	6♡
all pass			

Top-level Victory Point Swiss teams events nowadays often feature duplicated boards. This helps to avoid a situation in which you struggle to eke out a narrow 13-7 win on a series of dull boards only to find that your rivals have stormed past with a 20-0 score on a swingy set. It also means that you can compare results with a large number of other tables.

There are other ways to bid these two hands, of course, but a number of pairs reached 6♡. West generally led the ten of clubs and most of these slams went down. How do you think the successful declarers played?

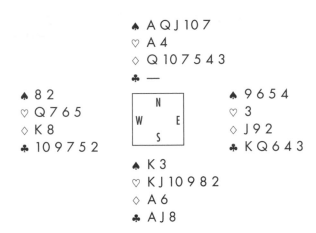

```
                    ♠ A Q J 10 7
                    ♡ A 4
                    ◇ Q 10 7 5 4 3
                    ♣ —
♠ 8 2                ┌─────────┐        ♠ 9 6 5 4
♡ Q 7 6 5            │    N    │        ♡ 3
◇ K 8              W │         │ E      ◇ J 9 2
♣ 10 9 7 5 2         │    S    │        ♣ K Q 6 4 3
                    └─────────┘
                    ♠ K 3
                    ♡ K J 10 9 8 2
                    ◇ A 6
                    ♣ A J 8
```

You play in 6♡ and West leads the ten of clubs.

In a teams event some declarers ruffed the club in dummy, unblocked the ace of hearts, crossed to the king of spades and laid down the king of hearts. Unfortunately, West was able to win the next heart and return a spade, reducing declarer to the hope that West held four spades as well as four hearts.

Ruffing two clubs in dummy is no better. Indeed, it actually worsens your chance of making the slam. Now you might go down even on a 3-2 trump break.

One well-known expert thought of a safety play: he won the opening lead in hand with the ace and ran the jack of hearts. His intention was to lose to the queen of hearts whilst a trump remained in dummy to deal with a club continuation. Again, the 4-1 trump split break proved too great an obstacle.

The solution is so simple that you will kick yourself if you have not seen it by now. Ruff the first club with the *ace* of hearts. Barring freak distribution you will be able to knock out the queen of hearts, draw trumps and discard three losers in the minor suits on dummy's spades.

Right Choice in Spades

```
              ♠ A Q 5
              ♡ K 7 6 4
              ◊ 8 6 5
              ♣ Q J 5

              ┌─────────┐
              │    N    │
♠ J led       │ W     E │
              │    S    │
              └─────────┘

              ♠ 6 2
              ♡ A J 10 9 8 5 3
              ◊ K 3
              ♣ A 2
```

Dealer South
E–W vul.

WEST	NORTH	EAST	SOUTH
			1♡
dbl	2NT	pass	4♡
all pass			

After West's takeout double North's 2NT indicates a hand with the values to raise to at least 3♡. (A bid of 3♡ would be preemptive, suggesting a hand on which he would have raised to only 2♡ without the double.)

West leads the jack of spades and you appear to have a number of chances to make the contract. Nevertheless, when this deal originally occurred the declarer went down, counting himself very unlucky. Would you have done any better?

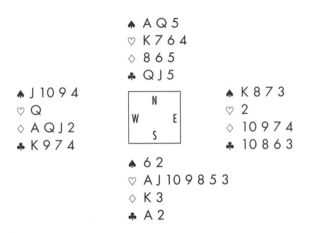

♠ A Q 5
♡ K 7 6 4
◇ 8 6 5
♣ Q J 5

♠ J 10 9 4
♡ Q
◇ A Q J 2
♣ K 9 7 4

♠ K 8 7 3
♡ 2
◇ 10 9 7 4
♣ 10 8 6 3

♠ 6 2
♡ A J 10 9 8 5 3
◇ K 3
♣ A 2

You play in 4♡ and West, who has doubled the 1♡ opening for takeout, leads the jack of spades.

The original declarer tried the queen of spades on the jack but East produced the king — losing finesse number one. East returned a diamond up to the weakness in dummy and declarer put up the king. West won with the ace — second keycard off-side — and a subsequent club finesse also failed.

'It's just my luck to find three cards wrong,' wailed South.

'I'm not so sure,' North observed. 'Once East turned up with the king of spades, West was likely to hold the other cards for his vulnerable double. Besides, if you'd made the right choice in spades then you wouldn't have needed any luck.

'You should duck the first round completely. East cannot overtake without setting up the queen as a discard for your losing club. After the jack wins and West plays a second spade, you can put up the ace and later take the club finesse into the safe West hand. Then you will be able to discard a diamond on the third round of clubs.'

Note that to play dummy's ace on the jack is not quite good enough. When the club finesse loses, West will be able to put his partner in with the king of spades to lead a diamond through.

One out of Four

```
        ♠ 10 3
        ♡ A J 8 5
        ◇ A J 7
        ♣ A K J 2
```

♣ 5 led

```
        ┌─────────┐
        │    N    │
        │ W     E │
        │    S    │
        └─────────┘
```

```
        ♠ A Q
        ♡ K Q 10 3
        ◇ K 8 5
        ♣ Q 10 8 3
```

Dealer East
Both vul.

WEST	NORTH	EAST	SOUTH
		pass	1NT
pass	2♣	pass	2♡
pass	6♡	all pass	

In a four-table team game, all four North-South pairs bid to 6♡, played by South. (At the tables where they were using a weak notrump and four-card majors, South still became declarer by opening 1♡.) We have given you the simplest auction, with a strong notrump opening and Stayman.

West leads a club and, assuming East cannot ruff, making the contract will present a problem only if West holds the king of spades and East the queen of diamonds. Can you see anything better than taking two finesses?

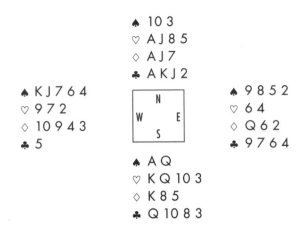

```
                    ♠ 10 3
                    ♡ A J 8 5
                    ◇ A J 7
                    ♣ A K J 2
♠ K J 7 6 4          ┌─────────┐          ♠ 9 8 5 2
♡ 9 7 2              │    N    │          ♡ 6 4
◇ 10 9 4 3         W │       E │          ◇ Q 6 2
♣ 5                  │    S    │          ♣ 9 7 6 4
                     └─────────┘
                    ♠ A Q
                    ♡ K Q 10 3
                    ◇ K 8 5
                    ♣ Q 10 8 3
```

South played in 6♡ at all the tables in a four-table team game. However, only once did the contract make.

'At our table declarer took two finesses and cursed his luck when both failed,' reported East at table one.

'I gave myself an extra chance but it didn't do me any good,' said South at table two. 'I drew trumps, eliminated the clubs and played three rounds of diamonds. If West had held the queen of diamonds he would have been endplayed, forced to lead a spade into the ace-queen or give a ruff and discard. I had the extra chance of a doubleton queen of diamonds.'

'They tried a variation on that at our table,' volunteered West at table three. 'Declarer eliminated the hearts and clubs, cashed the diamond king and played two rounds of spades. He must have been hoping for a 6-1 break or, of course, for one of the key-cards to sit right. If I didn't have the spade king and a second diamond we would have been done for.'

'I made the slam,' beamed South at table four. 'I too saw the advantage of the elimination play but I didn't touch diamonds at all. I exited with ace and queen of spades, forcing West to open up the diamonds. He did well to underlead his 10-9 but I let the diamond come around to my hand and up popped East's queen. I'm sure mine was the best line, and it worked!'

Italian Job

```
        ♠ K 6
        ♡ K Q 5
        ◇ K 9 7 5 4 2
        ♣ 5 4
```

```
          ┌─────┐
          │  N  │
♡J led    │ W  E│
          │  S  │
          └─────┘
```

```
        ♠ A 10 7
        ♡ A 7 6
        ◇ A 8
        ♣ Q J 7 3 2
```

Dealer South
N–S vul.

WEST	NORTH	EAST	SOUTH
			1NT[1]
2♡	3NT	all pass	

1. 15-17

Although the current Italian squad has not enjoyed quite as much success on the world stage as the legendary Blue Team, they have dominated the European scene for quite a few years, winning five consecutive European Championships.

On this deal, from a tournament on the continent, most of the declarers went down. (You will see why in a minute.) One of the few successful ones was one of our latter-day Italian heroes. (Sorry, our records do not indicate which one.)

Assuming IMP scoring, as is usual at teams, how should you play 3NT on a heart lead?

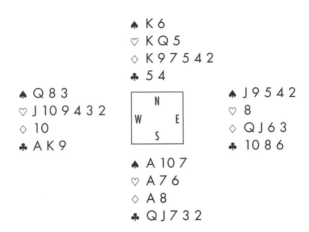

```
              ♠ K 6
              ♡ K Q 5
              ◇ K 9 7 5 4 2
              ♣ 5 4
♠ Q 8 3              ┌──────────┐              ♠ J 9 5 4 2
♡ J 10 9 4 3 2      │    N     │              ♡ 8
◇ 10                │ W      E │              ◇ Q J 6 3
♣ A K 9             │    S     │              ♣ 10 8 6
                    └──────────┘
              ♠ A 10 7
              ♡ A 7 6
              ◇ A 8
              ♣ Q J 7 3 2
```

South, who has opened a strong notrump, plays in 3NT. West, who has overcalled in hearts, leads the jack of hearts.

Most declarers went down by playing ace and a small diamond and ducking in dummy. With no heart left to return, the East players had no difficulty finding the club switch. This normally enabled the defenders to score three clubs and two diamonds because East got in twice to play clubs. Accidents only occurred when East foolishly won with the diamond queen. If this happened, West thought the diamonds were running, and so reckoned there was a rush to take club tricks.

Our Italian saw that he could almost certainly afford to lose two diamonds provided East didn't get in twice. Accordingly, he won the first heart on the table and led a diamond to the eight. East had to play low, and West won with the singleton ten and decided to persevere with another heart. Declarer won in hand, unblocked the ace of diamonds, crossed to dummy with the king of spades and cleared the diamonds. He was then able to cross back to the table with a heart and enjoy the rest of the diamonds. Thanks to his care in the timing of the safety play in diamonds, it would have taken ◇Q-J-10-x-(x) in the East hand to defeat him.

Twelve on Top

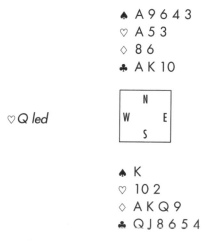

♠ A 9 6 4 3
♡ A 5 3
◇ 8 6
♣ A K 10

♡ Q *led*

♠ K
♡ 10 2
◇ A K Q 9
♣ Q J 8 6 5 4

Dealer East
Both vul.

WEST	NORTH	EAST	SOUTH
		3♠	4♣
pass	6♣	all pass	

For many centuries and certainly since Queen Elizabeth I of England ordered the execution of her cousin, Mary Queen of Scots, intense rivalry has existed between England and Scotland. This manifests itself in any sporting contest and in the fact that most people from South of the border consider themselves British first and English second while many from North of it regard themselves as Scottish first and foremost.

On this deal from an England/Scotland Camrose match, both Souths declared 6♣. Winning the first heart, they tried a trump and found East void. The bidding and lead mark the spades 7-0, but going down with twelve tricks there on top (as happened at one table) would be a pity, wouldn't it?

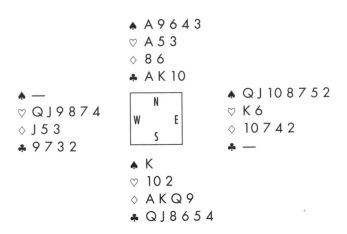

                    ♠ A 9 6 4 3
                    ♡ A 5 3
                    ◊ 8 6
                    ♣ A K 10
    ♠ —   ♠ Q J 10 8 7 5 2
    ♡ Q J 9 8 7 4   ♡ K 6
    ◊ J 5 3   ◊ 10 7 4 2
    ♣ 9 7 3 2   ♣ —
                    ♠ K
                    ♡ 10 2
                    ◊ A K Q 9
                    ♣ Q J 8 6 5 4

South is declarer in 6♣. After winning the heart lead, the Englishman tried a trump and found East void. The 4-0 trump split precluded a diamond ruff and, ironically, he could see nothing better than to finesse the ◊9, hoping East held ◊J-10-x-x. His counterpart, Hugh Kelsey, saw a way to succeed if East had any four diamonds.

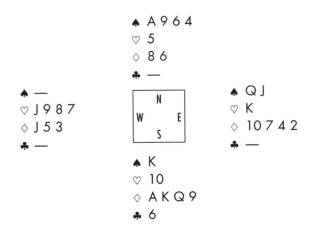

                    ♠ A 9 6 4
                    ♡ 5
                    ◊ 8 6
                    ♣ —
    ♠ —   ♠ Q J
    ♡ J 9 8 7   ♡ K
    ◊ J 5 3   ◊ 10 7 4 2
    ♣ —   ♣ —
                    ♠ K
                    ♡ 10
                    ◊ A K Q 9
                    ♣ 6

Kelsey ran all his trumps and East had to part with the ♡K to prevent declarer from overtaking the ♠K with the ace or running the diamonds. So next came the ♠K and then four rounds of diamonds. Now East had to lead a spade to dummy's ace.

Ominous Lead

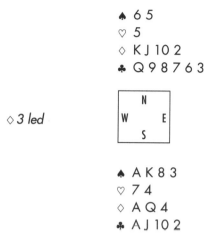

♠ 6 5
♡ 5
◇ K J 10 2
♣ Q 9 8 7 6 3

◇ 3 led

N
W   E
S

♠ A K 8 3
♡ 7 4
◇ A Q 4
♣ A J 10 2

Dealer South
Both vul.

WEST	NORTH	EAST	SOUTH
			1♣
1♡	4♣	4♡	4♠
pass	5♣	all pass	

Our correspondent, who wishes us to refer to him simply as John, tells us that this deal occurred in the round of sixteen of Crockfords, England's premier team event. Furthermore, John tells us that if he had made this contract, then his team would have progressed to the final. (That would have been the next round, as eight teams contest the final.)

Even facing a possible three-card suit, North's raise to 4♣ seems reasonable and we agree with South's 4♠ cuebid too.

How do you think declarer should play after West's ominous three of diamonds lead?

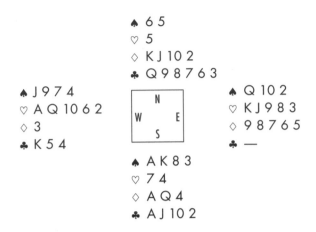

```
                    ♠ 6 5
                    ♡ 5
                    ◇ K J 10 2
                    ♣ Q 9 8 7 6 3
  ♠ J 9 7 4                              ♠ Q 10 2
  ♡ A Q 10 6 2        N                  ♡ K J 9 8 3
  ◇ 3              W      E               ◇ 9 8 7 6 5
  ♣ K 5 4              S                  ♣ —
                    ♠ A K 8 3
                    ♡ 7 4
                    ◇ A Q 4
                    ♣ A J 10 2
```

South plays in 5♣ after East-West have competed to 4♡. Neither defender has bid the suit, but West leads the three diamonds.

Most people lead 'MUD' or 'top-of-nothing' from small cards and John had little difficulty reading the opening lead as a singleton. Therefore, to keep the danger of an adverse ruff to a minimum, he decided not to take the trump finesse but to start by cashing the ace. In practice, East showed out on the first round of trumps and the question of finessing did not arise. John now saw that if he knocked out the king of clubs West would put his partner in with a heart and score a ruff.

In the hope West held ♠Q-J-10 (or would fail to unblock with a weaker holding), John played three rounds of spades, planning to throw dummy's singleton heart on the third round and sever the link between the defenders. Sadly, it was not to be.

John had the right idea, but he needed to play spades before touching trumps. Then he could have ruffed the third round, come to hand with the ace of clubs and played a fourth round. This way the Scissors Coup would work any time West has four spades or, of course, if he plays the highest outstanding spade on the third round.

fair Swap

```
        ♠ A
        ♡ 8 6 5 2
        ◊ Q 9 2
        ♣ 10 6 4 3 2
```

♣J led

```
        ♠ J 9 5 3
        ♡ K Q J 10 9 3
        ◊ A 8
        ♣ K
```

Dealer East
Neither vul.

WEST	NORTH	EAST	SOUTH
		1♣	1♡
1♠[1]	2♡	2♠	4♡
all pass			

1. Five or more spades. (Double would show only four).

West leads the jack of clubs against 4♡. East wins with the ace and switches to the seven of hearts.

You can assume that West is about to play ace and another trump, else you could ruff three spades in dummy and easily make ten tricks. If West does have the ace of trumps, it is highly likely that East holds the king of diamonds for his opening bid. This means that scoring a trick with dummy's queen will require some ingenuity. How do you set about it?

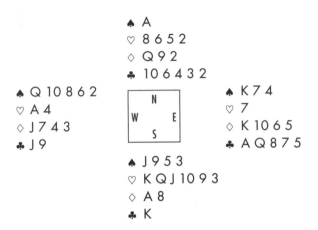

```
                 ♠ A
                 ♡ 8 6 5 2
                 ◊ Q 9 2
                 ♣ 10 6 4 3 2
♠ Q 10 8 6 2      ┌─────────┐    ♠ K 7 4
♡ A 4             │    N    │    ♡ 7
◊ J 7 4 3         │ W     E │    ◊ K 10 6 5
♣ J 9             │    S    │    ♣ A Q 8 7 5
                 └─────────┘
                 ♠ J 9 5 3
                 ♡ K Q J 10 9 3
                 ◊ A 8
                 ♣ K
```

You play in 4♡. The defenders, having begun with the jack of clubs to the ace, switch to trumps.

East might hold ♠K-Q-x, in which case two ruffs will make your jack good (and West may hold the ◊K after all). If not, you will surely need a throw-in for your tenth trick.

If East holds ♠Q-10-x or ♠K-10-x, or fails to unblock with ♠Q-x-x or ♠K-x-x, you can achieve a pretty elimination. Win the second trump in either hand, unblock the ♠A, ruff a club, ruff a spade, then play a third round of spades, pitching a diamond from dummy. After winning this trick East will face the unhappy choice of leading a club from the queen, allowing you to discard a diamond on dummy's ♣10, or playing from the ◊K, setting up dummy's queen as a winner.

On the actual layout, East can thwart this plan by jettisoning the king of spades either under the ace or, more likely, when you ruff the second round of spades. The solution is to start by playing a high heart so that you can win the second trump in dummy. Then ruff a club, cash the ace of spades and crossruff the next four tricks in the black suits. Finally you put East in with the last club, throwing a spade. With nothing but diamonds left, he must surrender a trick to dummy's queen.

No Overkill

♠ A Q J 8 5 4
♡ A 9 4
◇ A K
♣ 7 2

♡ 2 led

```
      N
   W     E
      S
```

♠ —
♡ J 7 6 5 3
◇ 8 6 5 4 3
♣ A K 5

Dealer North
Both vul.

WEST	NORTH	EAST	SOUTH
	1♠	pass	1NT
pass	3NT	all pass	

North had a tricky rebid and we agree with his choice, as nine
tricks can be easier than ten. For sure, 2NT and 3♠ hardly do his
hand justice, and jumping to three of a red suit would be fraught
with danger. Imagine what you would have done, with five-card
support for his supposed second suit!

Since you are playing for money, partner won't be at all
happy if you go down in 3NT with a combined 26 points. What
is your plan after West leads a small heart?

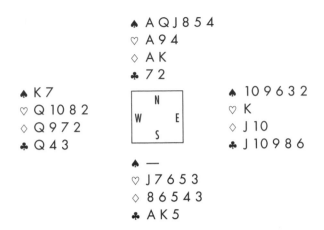

```
              ♠ A Q J 8 5 4
              ♡ A 9 4
              ◇ A K
              ♣ 7 2
♠ K 7                          ♠ 10 9 6 3 2
♡ Q 10 8 2      ┌─────────┐    ♡ K
◇ Q 9 7 2       │    N    │    ◇ J 10
♣ Q 4 3         │ W     E │    ♣ J 10 9 8 6
                │    S    │
                └─────────┘
              ♠ —
              ♡ J 7 6 5 3
              ◇ 8 6 5 4 3
              ♣ A K 5
```

You play in 3NT after responding 1NT to North's opening bid of
1♠. West leads the two of hearts.

All the textbooks tell you to begin your plan in a notrump
contract by counting your top tricks, and this approach should
save you from going astray here. With only six top tricks, you
need three more. So, if you play on a red suit and find a friendly
break, you will still need a second spade trick, and there may not
be the time or the communications for that. In any case, West's
decision to lead a heart reduces the chance of a 3-2 break in the
suit and a 3-3 diamond split is obviously against the odds.

The count on your top tricks also helps you decide how to
play the spades. If you needed five tricks, you would have no
choice but to play from the top in the hope that someone held
♠10-9-x or ♠K-10-9. In the actual scenario, four spade tricks will
suffice.

Any sensible approach will yield four spade tricks on a 4-3
break. To take advantage of a doubleton king, however, you must
force the defender who holds the king to play it on a small card.
So, either cash the ace and duck a spade or duck the first round.
Finally, since you don't want to risk an early club switch, you
should begin by putting up the ace of hearts.

Sixes and Sevens

♠ Q 9 5
♡ 9 7
◇ A K 8
♣ 10 9 6 5 2

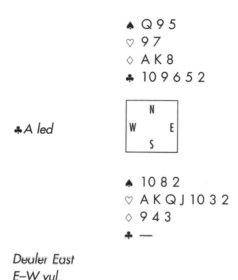

♣A led

♠ 10 8 2
♡ A K Q J 10 3 2
◇ 9 4 3
♣ —

Dealer East
E–W vul.

WEST	NORTH	EAST	SOUTH
		3♠	4♡
all pass			

You might casually observe that if West has a void in spades and all the top clubs, 3NT from your side of the table would be unbeatable. One could never, of course, expect to reach such a contract!

How do you intend to transform nine tricks into ten when West leads a top club against 4♡?

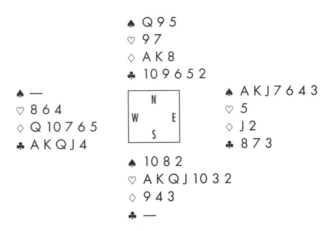

```
              ♠ Q 9 5
              ♡ 9 7
              ◇ A K 8
              ♣ 10 9 6 5 2
♠ —                              ♠ A K J 7 6 4 3
♡ 8 6 4          N               ♡ 5
◇ Q 10 7 6 5   W   E             ◇ J 2
♣ A K Q J 4        S             ♣ 8 7 3
              ♠ 10 8 2
              ♡ A K Q J 10 3 2
              ◇ 9 4 3
              ♣ —
```

You play in 4♡ after East has opened 3♠ in first seat. West leads
a top club.

As a singleton ♠J with West is most unlikely, your best hope
for a tenth trick lies in setting up a club winner. West has led a
club, but you still need four entries to dummy. The top diamonds and the ♡9 will provide three of these. Because you cannot readily force an opponent to lead clubs, the ♡7 will need to
be the fourth entry. It is more likely West has ♡8-x-x or similar
than that East has a lone eight, so you will finesse the seven.

If clubs break 4-4 and the trumps are not 4-0, you can simply
ruff four clubs high. Do you see how you can also succeed if East
has ♣8-7-x, ♣Q-8-7 or ♣J-8-7? After ruffing a club, finesse the ♡7
and lead the ♣10. When East plays the seven, you discard. West
does best to exit with a diamond, but you win in dummy and
lead the ♣9. When East plays the eight, you throw a spade. West
tries another diamond, but you win in dummy and the 6-5 have
become equals against his last high club. He has a trump left, but
this doesn't matter because he must follow to the fifth club.
Naturally, if East covers the ♣10 or ♣9 or you find out that he
can't have 8-7-x, Q-8-7 or J-8-7, you will ruff to keep him off play
and ensure dummy's second diamond entry stays intact.

Pointless Action

```
        ♠ 7 5
        ♡ K Q 10 8 6
        ◇ 9 7 6
        ♣ K Q J
```

```
                    ┌─────────┐
                    │    N    │
♠ 3 led             │ W     E │
                    │    S    │
                    └─────────┘
```

```
        ♠ A 9 8
        ♡ J 3
        ◇ A K 10
        ♣ A 8 5 4 3
```

Dealer East
E–W vul.

WEST	NORTH	EAST	SOUTH
		1♠	1NT
pass	2◇¹	pass	2♡
pass	3NT	all pass	

1. Transfer to hearts.

The bidding surely marks East with a five-card spade suit and the ace of hearts. Making 3NT is not going to be easy. You would have been better in 4♡.

West leads the three of spades and East plays the jack.

Since you are playing in a pairs competition, you might decide to hold up the ace of spades twice, planning to clear the hearts if spades are 5-3, settling for a probable one down. Alternatively, after checking that the clubs are not 5-0, you could finesse the ten of diamonds, playing East for the queen and jack. Can you see anything better than this?

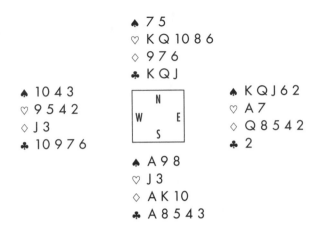

♠ 7 5
♡ K Q 10 8 6
◇ 9 7 6
♣ K Q J

♠ 10 4 3
♡ 9 5 4 2
◇ J 3
♣ 10 9 7 6

♠ K Q J 6 2
♡ A 7
◇ Q 8 5 4 2
♣ 2

♠ A 9 8
♡ J 3
◇ A K 10
♣ A 8 5 4 3

Playing this deal in 3NT, many declarers foolishly finessed the ◇10. This put them two down and was a pointless action anyway, since, if East did have ◇Q-J-x, a squeeze would have worked, one that also succeeds if he has any five diamonds. After you get in, unblock the clubs, cross to the ◇A and finish the clubs:

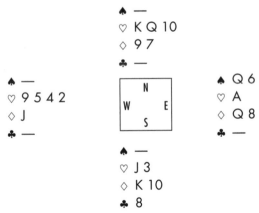

♠ —
♡ K Q 10
◇ 9 7
♣ —

♠ —
♡ 9 5 4 2
◇ J
♣ —

♠ Q 6
♡ A
◇ Q 8
♣ —

♠ —
♡ J 3
◇ K 10
♣ 8

On the last club, East can't discard his ace of hearts or another diamond without giving you a trick directly. After his forced spade discard, you can drive out the ♡A with impunity.

Guess Avoided

```
              ♠ A J 3
              ♡ A 8
              ◇ J 10 9 4 2
              ♣ Q 10 8

              ┌─────────┐
              │    N    │
  ♠ 4 led     │ W     E │
              │    S    │
              └─────────┘

              ♠ 8 6 5
              ♡ K Q J 7 4 3 2
              ◇ K 5
              ♣ A
```

Dealer North
Neither vul.

WEST	NORTH	EAST	SOUTH
	1NT[1]	pass	4♡
all pass			

1. 12-14

Best known now for his monthly column in *Bridge Plus* and his thriving class at the Southampton–Sutherland bridge club, Dave Huggett was once an International player. He and Mike Pomfrey (winner on 'Who Wants To Be A Millionaire?') played in the Camrose for England in the late 1970s.

As this deal from a recent league match shows, Huggett is no average performer. He managed to make 4♡ without having to guess the diamonds. How do you think he did it? (If you duck the first spade, East wins with the ten and returns the king.)

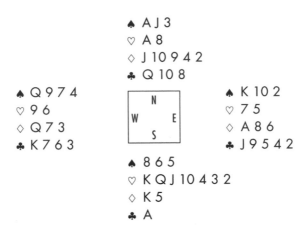

```
              ♠ A J 3
              ♡ A 8
              ◇ J 10 9 4 2
              ♣ Q 10 8
♠ Q 9 7 4         N           ♠ K 10 2
♡ 9 6                         ♡ 7 5
◇ Q 7 3     W         E       ◇ A 8 6
♣ K 7 6 3         S           ♣ J 9 5 4 2
              ♠ 8 6 5
              ♡ K Q J 10 4 3 2
              ◇ K 5
              ♣ A
```

South plays in 4♡ after North has opened a weak notrump. West leads the four of spades.

There are various ways to resolve the diamond position. Against some defenders, you do best to win the first spade and lead the jack of diamonds. For fear that you have a lone king, East might grab the ace of diamonds if he has it. Against someone who would expect you to play with greater subtlety if you really had a singleton king you might do better to draw trumps first. Another approach is to cash the ace of clubs, cross to dummy with a trump and advance the queen of clubs. This would enable you to test East's reflexes (if he has the king) but suffers from the drawback that the defenders are unlikely to place you with a singleton in both minors.

Dave Huggett did something else. He won the second round of spades, came to hand with a club and 'ran' the queen of hearts. Now, when he crossed to the ace of hearts and led the jack of diamonds from the table, East unhesitatingly went in with the ace! East presumed his partner began with K-9-6 of trumps, so envisaged four defensive tricks — two spades, a diamond and a trump. From East's point of view, South might have had a singleton ◇K in a 3-6-1-3 shape.

No Recovery

```
        ♠ K J 4
        ♡ Q 9 6 4 3 2
        ◇ 10 6 3
        ♣ A
```

```
              N
◇ Q led     W   E
              S
```

```
        ♠ A 8 2
        ♡ A 10 8 7 5
        ◇ K 5 2
        ♣ J 8
```

Dealer East
E–W vul.

WEST	NORTH	EAST	SOUTH
		1◇	1♡
pass	4♣	pass	4♡
all pass			

In the 'better minor' style, East's 1◇ promises a four-card suit unless his shape is precisely 4-4-3-2; he could have four clubs and four diamonds.

North's double jump to 4♣ is a splinter, indicating a raise to game with a singleton or void in clubs. (A single jump to 3♣ would be different: a fit-showing jump, with heart support and a source of tricks in clubs.)

West leads the queen of diamonds and this runs to the king. How do you play to escape the hideous possibility of losing one spade, one heart and two diamonds?

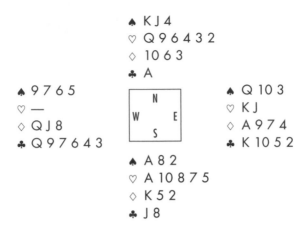

```
              ♠ K J 4
              ♡ Q 9 6 4 3 2
              ◇ 10 6 3
              ♣ A
♠ 9 7 6 5                            ♠ Q 10 3
♡ —              N                   ♡ K J
◇ Q J 8       W     E                ◇ A 9 7 4
♣ Q 9 7 6 4 3     S                  ♣ K 10 5 2
              ♠ A 8 2
              ♡ A 10 8 7 5
              ◇ K 5 2
              ♣ J 8
```

You play in 4♡. West, acting on his partner's opening bid of 1◇, leads the queen of diamonds, and this runs to the king.

If trumps break 2-0, you face an inevitable loser there, and it seems hard to avoid the loss of two diamonds. If East has the king and queen of clubs, he may hold sufficient strength for an opening bid without the queen of spades. In this case, a simple finesse will work, but you don't want to rely on this.

The symmetry of distribution suggests a throw-in, but you must take care in case West has the diamond jack. Suppose you start with a club to the ace. You cannot afford to play a heart to the ace yet (East could win the next diamond, cash the ♡K and lead a diamond to West's jack), so you will have to lead a diamond from dummy. Unfortunately, this allows West to get in twice and he will lead a spade each time to scupper your plan.

To succeed as the cards lie you need to play a diamond straight back. West can win on the second or third round of diamonds and lead a spade, but you can cope with that. You duck in dummy and win with the ace, unblock the club ace, return to the heart ace and ruff a club. A trump exit then forces East to lead a spade into the tenace or give a ruff and discard.

Added Protection

```
              ♠ A 6 3
              ♡ Q 5 4
              ◇ Q 8 4
              ♣ A 5 4 3

                    ┌──────┐
                    │   N  │
♠ 10 led            │ W  E │
                    │   S  │
                    └──────┘

              ♠ K 7 4
              ♡ A K 8 2
              ◇ A K J 10 2
              ♣ 6
```

Dealer South
Neither vul.

WEST	NORTH	EAST	SOUTH
			1◇
pass	2NT	pass	3♡
pass	3♠	pass	4♠
pass	6◇	all pass	

Without a natural 2NT response available, this might have been
a tricky slam to reach, as a 2♣ response might lead you to think
the hands were fitting poorly. As it was, North, having limited
his hand to 10-12 on the first round, was free to take an aggres-
sive stance later: queens in both of your suits and aces in the
other two were all great cards to have.

West leads the ten of spades against the diamond slam.
Bearing in mind that the chance (in a problem) of a 3-3 heart split
is lower than the usual 36%, how do you plan the play?

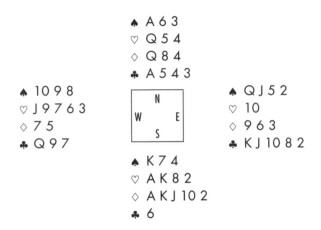

```
                  ♠ A 6 3
                  ♡ Q 5 4
                  ◊ Q 8 4
                  ♣ A 5 4 3
♠ 10 9 8          ┌─────────┐        ♠ Q J 5 2
♡ J 9 7 6 3       │    N    │        ♡ 10
◊ 7 5             │ W     E │        ◊ 9 6 3
♣ Q 9 7           │    S    │        ♣ K J 10 8 2
                  └─────────┘
                  ♠ K 7 4
                  ♡ A K 8 2
                  ◊ A K J 10 2
                  ♣ 6
```

You play in 6◊ and West leads a spade.

The flat dummy and singleton in your hand seem to suggest a dummy reversal, but a closer inspection reveals the problem with that. In order to ruff three clubs in hand and get back to dummy to draw the last trump, you will need four entries to dummy, which means finessing West for the ◊9.

A squeeze also sounds possible. If one defender has four hearts and five clubs or four hearts and five spades, you can exert some pressure. Indeed the same timing — give up one club and ruff another — should work in both cases, effectively playing a double squeeze, with hearts as the pivot suit.

We prefer, however, the simple plan of trying to ruff the fourth heart in dummy. This should prove easy enough if the defender with four hearts has trump length, but you can also do it if East has three trumps and short hearts. Put up the ♠A and draw two rounds of trumps with, say, the ace and jack. Then cross to the ♡Q and lead a heart to the ace. Go back to the ♣A and lead another heart. If nobody has ruffed, you ruff the fourth round of hearts with the ◊Q. If East ruffs the second or third heart, he ruffs a loser, and you can later discard a spade from dummy on a master heart and ruff a spade.

Interior Design

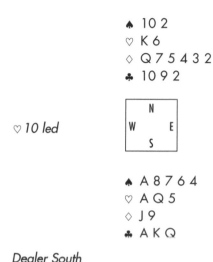

```
          ♠ 10 2
          ♡ K 6
          ◇ Q 7 5 4 3 2
          ♣ 10 9 2

                 N
♡ 10 led      W     E
                 S

          ♠ A 8 7 6 4
          ♡ A Q 5
          ◇ J 9
          ♣ A K Q
```

Dealer South
E–W vul.

WEST	NORTH	EAST	SOUTH
			2NT¹
pass	3NT	all pass	

1. 20-21

West leads the ten of hearts against the notrump game and you can see seven top tricks.

Should you try to develop dummy's diamonds or your own spades, or should you try to combine your chances? Also, if you decide to concentrate on one suit, does it matter which card you lead first?

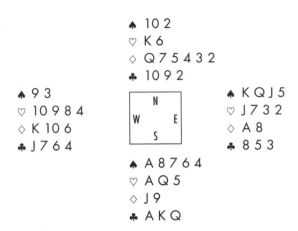

♠ 10 2
♡ K 6
◇ Q 7 5 4 3 2
♣ 10 9 2

♠ 9 3
♡ 10 9 8 4
◇ K 10 6
♣ J 7 6 4

♠ K Q J 5
♡ J 7 3 2
◇ A 8
♣ 8 5 3

♠ A 8 7 6 4
♡ A Q 5
◇ J 9
♣ A K Q

As South, you play in 3NT. West leads the ten of hearts.

You have seven tricks on top and need to develop two more. Dummy's assets include a six-card diamond suit, but a lack of entries surely makes it impossible to use the suit. Nor is there much point in trying to steal one diamond trick, since if you can make two spade tricks you can probably make three.

A 3-3 spade split would make life easy, and you can also handle K-9, Q-9 or J-9 with West if you lead low from hand. If he plays the nine, dummy's ten will force out a high card from East and cashing the ace next will leave the 8-7 as equals against East's other high spade. If West wins the first spade, you will use the ♡K as an entry to lead the ♠10 and pin the nine.

You may have an extra chance if West has ♠9-x. You lead a middle spade from hand, intending to let it run, and finesse against East on the next round. The snag is that if West plays the nine you won't know whether it is from 9-x (when you need to finesse next time) or from K-9, Q-9 or J-9 (when you want to cash the ace). The principle that you lead low when you don't want a cover applies here. If you lead the six, West can hardly play the nine from 9-x lest you hold A-K-8-6 or A-K-8-6-x. If he plays the nine 'to signal his doubleton', count yourself unlucky!

Safe Inference

```
            ♠ K Q J 5
            ♡ 10 5
            ◇ 10 5 2
            ♣ A J 5 2

                  ┌──────────┐
                  │    N     │
   ♡ 2 led        │ W      E │
                  │    S     │
                  └──────────┘

            ♠ A 9 8 4
            ♡ Q 3
            ◇ A Q 7
            ♣ K 10 9 4
```

Dealer South
N–S vul.

WEST	NORTH	EAST	SOUTH
			1NT
pass	2♣	pass	2♠
pass	4♠	all pass	

As South, you show 15-17 balanced, with four spades but not four hearts, and arrive in 4♠.

West leads the two of hearts. East cashes the king and ace before switching to a trump. You draw trumps in three rounds, ending in dummy, with West discarding a heart on the third.

You have lost two tricks and can't avoid losing a diamond. To avoid any further losers it looks like you will need to take a successful finesse in one minor and try for a throw-in to resolve the remaining position. How should you set about it?

                          ♠ K Q J 5
                          ♡ 10 5
                          ◊ 10 5 2
                          ♣ A J 5 2
    ♠ 10 2   ♠ 7 6 3
    ♡ J 9 7 2   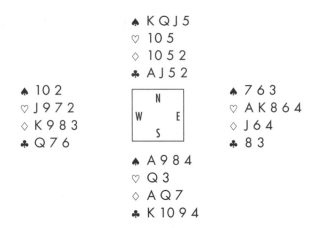   ♡ A K 8 6 4
    ◊ K 9 8 3   ◊ J 6 4
    ♣ Q 7 6   ♣ 8 3
                          ♠ A 9 8 4
                          ♡ Q 3
                          ◊ A Q 7
                          ♣ K 10 9 4

After a simple auction, you play in 4♠. East cashes two top
hearts and you draw trumps in three rounds.

   To take a diamond finesse would be a mistake. If it loses, you
will surely go down, and you are not out of the woods if it works.
Whoever wins the third round of the suit can afford to give a ruff
and discard, leaving you to guess the clubs.

   Since West holds four hearts (he led the two) to East's five
and two trumps to East's three, you should finesse West for the
♣Q. When this works, all comes down to the diamonds:

                          10 5 2
    K 9 8 3   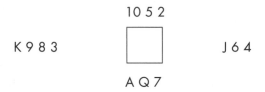   J 6 4
                          A Q 7

To lead the ten would be a mistake, losing whenever East holds
the jack and West the king. Instead, you lead low to the seven,
landing the contract easily as the cards lie. If East had the eight
or nine and played it, you would cover and know to let the next
diamond run around to hand as (a) it is twice as likely that East
was dealt J-9-x or J-8-x than 9-8-x and (b) without the ◊J East
would surely have led a diamond after cashing his hearts.

As Good as a Nod

```
                    ♠ 6 5
                    ♡ A 7 5 3
                    ◇ K 7 5 2
                    ♣ J 10 6

                    ┌─────────┐
                    │    N    │
    ♡ 6 led         │ W     E │
                    │    S    │
                    └─────────┘

                    ♠ A K Q J 10 3
                    ♡ 8
                    ◇ A Q 10 6
                    ♣ A 8
```

Dealer South
N–S vul.

WEST	NORTH	EAST	SOUTH
			2♣
2♡	2NT	3♡	3♠
pass	4♠	pass	6♠
all pass			

You might have reached 6◇ if North had bid 3NT at his second turn, but perhaps he worried that this would suggest wasted heart values. In any event, 6♠ looks a good contract, only in danger if West holds ◇J-x-x-x.

If West does have the guarded ◇J, you might think of a throw-in or a squeeze against him. The trouble is that unless East helpfully returns a heart (if you duck the opening lead) or throws a heart, he can guard the third round of the suit (West may need to unblock) and spoil the party. How do you plan the play?

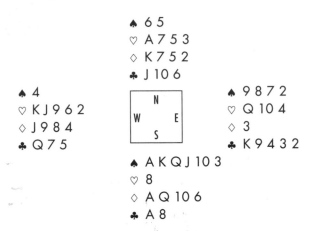

Provided West has the ♣K or ♣Q (or both), you can make 6♠ without relying on any error. Put up the ♡A, ruff a heart and pull four rounds of trumps to reduce to something like this:

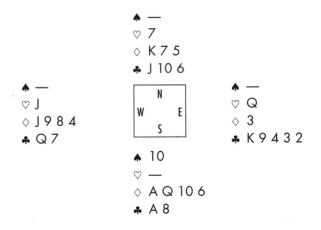

Then cash the ace-king of diamonds, getting the news, ruff a heart to hand and play the ♣A followed by another club. East can either leave West on play, forced to lead a diamond, or over-take with the king and surrender a club trick to dummy. This is a winkle squeeze, so named by Terence Reese.